The Alpha and Omega

"The straight testimony of the true Witness to Laodicea"

Michael R. Karr

We must adjust our theology to fit Scripture rather than adjusting Scripture to fit our theology, as the scribes and Pharisees did.

World rights reserved. This book or any portion thereof may not be copied or reproduced in any form or manner whatever, except as provided by law, without the written permission of the publisher, except by a reviewer who may quote brief passages in a review.

The author assumes full responsibility for the accuracy of all facts and quotations as cited in this book. The opinions expressed in this book are the author's personal views and interpretations, and do not necessarily reflect those of the publisher.

This book is provided with the understanding that the publisher is not engaged in giving spiritual, legal, medical, or other professional advice. If authoritative advice is needed, the reader should seek the counsel of a competent professional.

Emphasis in the scriptural quotations and other quotations is that of the author unless otherwise noted.

Copyright © 2023 Michael Karr
Copyright © 2023 TEACH Services, Inc.
ISBN-13: 978-1-4796-1502-5 (Paperback)
ISBN-13: 978-1-4796-1503-2 (ePub)
Library of Congress Control Number: 2022923845

All scripture quotations, unless otherwise indicated, are taken from the King James Version Bible. Public domain.

Scripture taken from the NEW AMERICAN STANDARD BIBLE (R), copyright (C) 1960, 1962, 1963, 1968, 1971, 1972, 1973, 1975, 1977, 1995 by The Lockman Foundation. Used by permission.

Cover Design by Joshua Knapp

ABBREVIATIONS

1SM	*Selected Messages, bk. 1*
5T	*Testimonies to the Church, vol. 5*
6T	*Testimonies to the Church, vol. 6*
8T	*Testimonies to the Church, vol. 8*
AA	*The Acts of the Apostles*
DA	*The Desire of Ages*
Ed	*Education*
EW	*Early Writings*
GC	*The Great Controversy*
LDE	*Last Day Events*
MB	*Thoughts From the Mount of Blessing*
MH	*The Ministry of Healing*
PK	*Prophets and Kings*
PP	*Patriarchs and Prophets*
TMK	*That I May Know Him*
UL	*The Upward Look*
YI	*The Youth's Instructor*

DEDICATION

To the following individuals, I dedicate this book.

- Chuck Smith
- Rupert Preddie
- Elder Bob Harris
- Pastor Gerry Fisher
- Pastor Monte Robison
- Pastor Walter Castro
- Elder Joe Fider
- Elder Oswald Vassell
- Pastor Leonard Kitson
- Adam Lawrence

Without the combined influence of these men's lives and the Holy Spirit, this book may never have been written. God bless each and every one of you!

PREFACE

The Remnant Church

God defines the remnant church in Revelation. "And the dragon was wroth with the woman, and went to make war with the remnant of her seed, which keep the commandments of God, and have the testimony of Jesus Christ" (Rev. 12:17). "… I am thy fellow servant, and of thy brethren that have the testimony of Jesus: worship God: for the testimony of Jesus is the spirit of prophecy" (Rev. 19:10).

Not only is the church defined by God in these texts, but the church defines herself by these texts. It is who we are—and it must continue to be—if we are to remain God's remnant church. This definition places obligations upon us by God for the gifts He has given us.

1. "The law of God, being a revelation of His will, a transcript of His character, must forever endure, 'as a faithful witness in heaven.' Not one command has been annulled; not a jot or tittle has been changed. [Matt. 5:18.] Says the psalmist: 'Forever, O Lord, Thy word is settled in heaven.' 'All His commandments are sure. They stand fast for ever and ever.' Psalm 119:89; 111:7, 8" (GC 434).

2. Ellen G. White's ministry is a gift that God has given Seventh-day Adventists. We *define* ourselves by her *historical presence* in our church, for her writings are the "Spirit of Prophecy" in this church (see Rev. 19:10). She is not something or someone that the church has moved past. She came to us as a signet from God to declare to the world who we are and who

> "The law of God, being a revelation of His will, a transcript of His character, must forever endure, 'as a faithful witness in heaven.'"

He is. She was also sent as Elijah to God's church to light the way at the end of time so we would not stumble and fall off the path. What she accomplished could not have been done without God's presence through His Holy Spirit. Her writings continue to speak to us regarding God's plans for this church. "Believe in the LORD your God, so shall ye be established; believe his prophets, so shall ye prosper" (2 Chron. 20:20).

Since the Spirit of Prophecy defines this church, isn't it odd that, instead of following *her* definition of *what the law is*, we have followed the definition given by Uriah Smith and G. I. Butler? See G. I. Butler's book, *The Law in the Book of Galatians*, and Uriah Smith's book, *What Was Nailed to the Cross?*

In one of her articles, she defines *the law of God*.

"In consequence of continual transgression, the *moral law* was repeated in awful grandeur from Sinai. Christ gave to Moses religious *precepts* which were to govern the everyday life. These *statutes were explicitly given to guard the ten commandments*. They were not shadowy types to pass away with the death of Christ. They were to be *binding upon man* in every age *as long as time should last*. These commands were enforced by the power of the moral law, and they clearly and definitely explained that law.

"*Moses of himself framed no law*. Christ, the angel whom God had appointed to go before his chosen people, gave to Moses statutes and requirements necessary to a living religion and to govern the people of God. Christians commit a terrible mistake in calling this law severe and arbitrary, and then contrasting it with the gospel and mission of Christ in his ministry on earth, as though he were in opposition to the just precepts which they call the law of Moses.

> "Christians commit a terrible mistake in calling this law severe and arbitrary, and then contrasting it with the gospel and mission of Christ in his ministry on earth, as though he were in opposition to the just precepts which they call the law of Moses."

"The law of Jehovah, dating back to creation, was comprised in the two great principles, 'Thou shalt love the Lord thy God with all thy heart, and with all thy soul, and with all thy mind, and with all thy strength. This is the first commandment. And the second is like, namely this: Thou shalt love thy neighbor as thyself. There is none other commandment greater than these.' These two great principles embrace the first four commandments, showing the duty of man to God, and the last six, showing the duty of man to his fellow-man. The principles were more explicitly stated to man after the fall, and worded to meet the case of fallen intelligences. This was necessary in consequence of the minds of men being blinded by transgression.

"God graciously spoke his law and wrote it with his own finger on stone, making a solemn covenant with his people at Sinai. God acknowledged them as his peculiar treasure above all people upon the earth. *Christ, who went before Moses in the wilderness, made the principles of morality and religion more clear by particular precepts, specifying the duty of man to God and his fellow-men, for the purpose of protecting life, and guarding the sacred law of God, that it should not be entirely forgotten in the midst of an apostate world.*

"Professed Christians now cry, Christ! Christ is our righteousness, but away with the law. They talk and act as though Christ's mission to a fallen world was for the express purpose of nullifying his Father's law. Could not that work have been just as well executed without the only beloved of the Father coming to this world and enduring grief, privation, and the shameful death of the cross? Ministers preach that the atonement gave men liberty to break the law of God, and to commit sin, and then praise the free grace and mercy revealed through Christ under the gospel, while they despise the law of God.

"They cast aside the restraint of the law, and give loose rein to the corrupt passions and the promptings of the natural heart, and then triumph in the mercy and grace of the gospel. Christ speaks to such: 'Not every one that saith unto me, Lord, Lord, shall enter into the kingdom of Heaven; but he that doeth the will of my Father which is in Heaven.' What is the will of the Father? That we keep his commandments. *Christ, to enforce the will of his Father, became the author of the statutes and precepts given through Moses to the people of God. Christians who extol Christ, but array themselves against the law governing the Jewish church, array Christ against Christ*" (*Review and Herald*, May 6, 1875, pars. 10, 12–6).

The church has railed against the popular Protestant belief that the law was nailed to the cross while, at the same time, nailing parts of the moral law to the cross that *we* don't want to keep.

Ellen White is quite specific, in her writings, regarding what was nailed to the cross. "He [God] communicated with Moses from the cloud of glory above the mercy seat, and gave him full directions concerning the *system of offerings* and the *forms of worship* to be maintained *in the sanctuary*. The ceremonial law was thus given to Moses, and by him written in a book. There are many who try to blend these two systems, using the texts that speak of the ceremonial law to prove that the moral law has been abolished; but this is a perversion of the Scriptures. The distinction between the two systems is broad and clear. The *ceremonial system was made up of symbols pointing to Christ*, to *His sacrifice* and *His priesthood*. This ritual law, with its sacrifices and ordinances, was to be performed by the Hebrews until type met antitype in the death of Christ, the Lamb of God that taketh away the sin of the world. Then all the *sacrificial offerings* were to cease. It is this law that Christ 'took ... out of the way, nailing it to His cross.' Colossians 2:14" (PP 364.3–365.1).

Note: The ceremonial law concerned the system of offerings, forms of worship in the sanctuary, and symbols pointing to Christ, His sacrifice, and His priesthood—*nothing else*!

In *The Bible Echo*, October 31, 1898, she states: "Christ passed through all the experiences of His *childhood, youth, and manhood* without the observance of ceremonial temple worship."

Everything Jesus practiced or taught serves as our example. God has left us a Book which Scripture and the Spirit of Prophecy state must be read as written.

"Many do not hesitate to sneer at the word of God. Those who believe that word just as it reads are held up to ridicule. There is a growing contempt for law and order, directly traceable to a violation of the plain commands of Jehovah. Violence and crime are the result of turning aside from the path of obedience. Behold the wretchedness and misery of multitudes who worship at the shrine of idols and who seek in vain for happiness and peace" (PK 185.2).

"The prevailing spirit of our time is one of infidelity and apostasy—a spirit of avowed illumination because of a knowledge of truth, but in reality of the blindest presumption. Human theories are exalted and placed where God and His law should be. Satan tempts men and women to disobey, with the promise that in disobedience they will find liberty and freedom that will make them as gods. There is seen a spirit of opposition to the plain word of God, of idolatrous exaltation of human wisdom above divine revelation. Men have allowed their minds to become so darkened and confused by conformity to worldly customs and influences that they seem to have lost all power to discriminate between light and darkness, truth and error. So far have they departed from the right way that they hold the opinions of a few philosophers, so-called, to be more trustworthy than the truths of the Bible. The entreaties and promises of God's word, its threatenings against disobedience and *idolatry*—these seem powerless to melt their hearts. A faith such as actuated Paul, Peter, and John they regard as old-fashioned, mystical, and unworthy of the intelligence of modern thinkers" (PK 178.1).

Commenting on Revelation 22:18, 19, Ellen White wrote: "Such are the warnings which God has given to guard men against changing in any manner that which He has revealed or commanded. These solemn denunciations apply to all who by their influence lead men to regard lightly the law of God. *They should cause those to fear and tremble who flippantly declare it a matter of little consequence whether we obey God's law or not. All who exalt their own opinions above divine revelation, all who would change the plain meaning of Scripture to suit their own convenience, or for the sake of conforming to the world, are taking upon themselves a fearful responsibility.* The *written word*, the *law of God*, will measure the character of every man and condemn all whom this unerring test shall declare wanting" (GC 268.2).

When Christ came the first time, He said, "Woe unto you, scribes and Pharisees, hypocrites! for ye pay tithe of mint and anise and cummin, and have omitted the weightier matters of the law, judgment, mercy, and faith: these ought ye to have done, and not to leave the other undone" (Matt. 23:23). What Jesus came teaching was the Mosaic law, which was the kinder, gentler side of the law—laws that look out for the weak and helpless among us, that talk of our relationship with the Father and the time we spend with Him, and that warn us of the consequences of rebellion against His law.

"Whenever the study of the Scriptures is entered upon without a prayerful, humble, teachable spirit, the plainest and simplest as well as the most difficult passages will be wrested from their true meaning. The papal leaders select such portions of Scripture as best serve their purpose, interpret to suit themselves, and then present these to the people, while they deny them the privilege of studying the Bible and understanding its sacred truths for themselves. *The whole Bible should be given to the people just as it reads.* It would be better for them not to have Bible instruction at all than to have the teaching of the Scriptures thus grossly misrepresented" (GC 521.2).

"The truths most plainly revealed in the Bible have been involved in doubt and darkness by learned men, who, with a pretense of great wisdom, teach that the Scriptures have a mystical, a secret, spiritual meaning not apparent in the language employed. These men are false teachers. It was to such a class that Jesus declared: 'Ye know not the Scriptures, neither the power of God.' Mark 12:24. The language of the Bible should be explained according to its obvious meaning, unless a symbol or figure is employed.

"Christ has given the promise: 'If any man will do His will, he shall know of the doctrine.' John 7:17. If men would but take the Bible as it reads, if there were no false teachers to mislead and confuse their minds, a work would be accomplished that would make angels glad and that would bring into the fold of Christ thousands upon thousands who are now wandering in error" (GC 598.3).

"God requires more of His followers than many realize. If we would not build our hopes of heaven upon a false foundation we must accept the Bible as it reads and believe that the Lord means what He says. He requires nothing of us that He will not give us grace to perform. We shall have no excuse to offer in the day of God if we fail to reach the standard set before us in His word" (5T 171.1).

Church officials who cast off the *Review and Herald* article on the "Law of God" from 1875 as just seventeen paragraphs do so at the peril of their souls and at the peril of the souls of those whom they pastor, teach, lead, guide, and disciple. Not accepting what Ellen White tells us of the law of God is one thing, but to stand in the way of others hearing it is something else. "But whoso shall *offend* [Greek, *skandalizō*, "trap, trip up, stumble, entice to sin," G4624] one of these little ones which believe in me, it were better for him that a millstone were hanged about his neck, and that he were drowned in the depth of the sea" (Matt. 18:6).

"And it came to pass, that when Jehudi had read three or four leaves, he cut it with the penknife, and cast it into the fire that was on the hearth, until all the roll was consumed in the fire that was on the hearth. Yet they were not afraid, nor rent their garments, neither the king, nor any of his servants that heard all these words" (Jer. 36:23, 24).

However, that could not be what we are doing, *right*?

"Therefore have I also made you contemptible and base before all the people, according as ye have not kept my ways, *but have been partial in the law*" (Mal. 2:9).

"Every mind should turn with reverent attention to the revealed word of God. Light and grace will be given to those who thus obey God. They will behold wondrous things out of *his law*. Great truths that have lain unheeded and unseen since the day of Pentecost, are to shine from God's word in their native purity. To those who truly love God the Holy Spirit will reveal truths that have faded from the mind, and will also reveal truths that are entirely new" (*The Ellen G. White 1888 Materials*, p. 1651, par. 8).

INTRODUCTION

"*There is no excuse for any one in taking the position that there is no more truth to be revealed, and that all our expositions of Scripture are without an error. The fact that certain doctrines have been held as truth for many years by our people, is not a proof that our ideas are infallible.* Age will not make error into truth, and truth can afford to be fair. No true doctrine will lose anything by close investigation. We are living in perilous times, and it does not become us to accept everything claimed to be truth without examining it thoroughly; neither can we afford to reject anything that bears the fruits of the Spirit of God; but we should be teachable, meek and lowly of heart. There are those who oppose everything that is not in accordance with their own ideas, and by so doing they endanger their eternal interest as verily as did the Jewish nation in their rejection of Christ. The Lord designs that our opinions shall be put to the test, that we may see the necessity of closely examining the living oracles to see whether or not we are in the faith. Many who claim to believe the truth have settled down at their ease [Zeph. 1:12], saying, 'I am rich, and increased with goods, and have need of nothing.' But Jesus says to these self-complacent ones, *Thou 'knowest not that thou art wretched, and miserable, and poor, and blind, and naked.'* Let us individually inquire, Do these words describe my case? If so, the True Witness counsels us, saying, 'Buy of me gold tried in the fire, that thou mayest be rich; and white raiment, that thou mayest be clothed, that the shame of thy nakedness do not appear; and anoint thine eyes with eye-salve, that thou mayest see.' [Rev. 3:17, 18].

"From the description of the Laodiceans, it is evident that many were deceived in their estimate of their spiritual condition. They regarded themselves as rich, as *possessing* all the *knowledge* and *grace* that was needed; but yet they *lacked* the *gold of faith* and *love*, the white raiment of Christ's righteousness" (*Review and Herald*, Dec. 20, 1892, par. 1, 2).

Regarding the outpouring of the Spirit and the truth He brings, she says: "In the manifestation of that power which lightens the earth with the glory of God, they will see only something which, in their blindness they think dangerous, something which will arouse their fears, and they will brace themselves to resist it. Because the Lord does not work according to their expectations and ideal, they will oppose the work. 'Why,' they say, 'should we not know the Spirit of God, when we have been in the work so many years?' Because they did not respond to the warnings, the entreaties, of the messages of God, but persistently said, 'I am rich, and increased with goods, and have need of nothing' " (*Maranatha*, p. 219, par. 2).

"Every soul is to put himself to the task of searching out the truth as it is in Jesus, to know it for himself by the study of the sure word of God. We are not to ask, What is the popular opinion? What saith brother A. or brother B. or any other man? What saith the fathers? But what saith the Lord our God in regard to the saving of the soul? And when we have found what saith the Scriptures, *let us act upon the written word*; for it is perilous to sit in judgment on the words of inspiration. That which has been written is for our instruction, admonition, and comfort.

"No works that the sinner can do will be efficacious in saving his soul. Obedience was always due to the Creator; for he endowed man with attributes for his service. God requires good works from man always; but good works cannot avail to earn salvation. It is impossible for man to save himself. He may deceive himself in regard to this matter; but he cannot save himself. Christ's righteousness alone can avail for his salvation, and this is the gift of God. This is the wedding garment prepared for you in which you may be a welcome guest at the marriage supper of the Lamb. Let faith take hold of Christ without delay, and you will be a new creature in Jesus, a light to the world" (*Review and Herald*, Dec. 20, 1892, par. 8, 12).

"*The Reformation did not, as many suppose, end with Luther. It is to be continued to the close of this world's history. Luther had a great work to do in reflecting to others the light which God had permitted to shine upon him; yet he did not receive all the light which was to be given to the world. From that time to this, new light has been continually shining upon the Scriptures, and new truths have been constantly unfolding*" (GC 148).

"There are glorious truths to come before the people of God. *Privileges and duties* which they do not even suspect to be in the Bible will be laid open before the followers of Christ. As they follow on in the path of humble obedience, doing God's will, they will know more and more of the *oracles* of God, and be established in right *doctrines*" (TMK 114.5; see also John 7:17; Heb. 5:9; Col. 3:12, 13, 16, 17).

"*The experience of these noble Reformers contains a lesson for all succeeding ages. Satan's manner of working against God and His word has not changed; he is still as much opposed to the Scriptures being made the guide of life as in the sixteenth century. In our time there is a wide departure from their doctrines and precepts, and there is need of a return to the great Protestant principle—the Bible, and the Bible only, as the rule of faith and duty. Satan is still working through every means which he can control to destroy religious liberty*" (GC 204.2).

> "There are glorious truths to come before the people of God. Privileges and duties which they do not even suspect to be in the Bible will be laid open before the followers of Christ."

"If any man will do his will, he shall know of the doctrine, whether it be of God, or whether I speak of myself" (John 7:17).

CONTENTS

Preface	v
Introduction	xi
Chapter 1. The Truth	19
Chapter 2. The Law and Salvation	29
A. Grace	30
B. Faith	30
C. The Sacrifice of Christ	30
D. Leadership and the Law	34
E. The Spirit and the Law	35
F. Coming to Christ	36
G. Putting It All Together	36
Chapter 3. The Law of Moses	38
A. The Ceremonial Law	39
B. The Moral Law	41
Chapter 4. The New Covenant	44
Chapter 5. The Curses	49
A. Moses and the Curses	50
B. Isaiah and the Curses	50
C. Zechariah and the Curses	51
D. Josiah and the Curses—The Curses in Chronicles	53
E. Nehemiah and the Curses	54
F. Jesus Speaks of the Curses	55

Chapter 6. Who Kept the Statutes? ... 56
   A. Abraham ... 56
   B. Joseph ... 57
   C. Moses ... 57
   D. Joshua ... 59
   E. David ... 60
   F. Isaiah ... 60
   G. Josiah ... 61
   H. Jeremiah ... 61
   I. Daniel ... 61
   J. Ezekiel ... 62
   K. Ezra ... 62
   L. Nehemiah ... 63
   M. Hosea ... 63
   N. Amos ... 63
   O. Zechariah ... 64
   P. Zephaniah ... 64
   O. Malachi ... 64
   R. Jesus ... 65
   S. Paul ... 67
   T. James ... 70
   U. Jude ... 70
   V. John ... 71

Chapter 7. What Was *Not* Nailed to the Cross ... 72

Chapter 8. The Cost of Not Keeping the Commandments, Statutes, and Judgments ... 78

Chapter 9. The Sins of Jeroboam ... 81

Chapter 10. The Elijah Message ... 84

Chapter 11. The Feasts ... 90
   A. What Are *Moeds*? ... 93
   B. The Sabbath and the Other Feasts ... 96
      1. Sabbath ... 79

2. Passover	81
3. Unleavened Bread	82
4. Pentecost—Feast of Weeks	84
5. Trumpets	85
6. Atonement	86
7. Tabernacles	87
Chapter 12. The Sabbath of the Seventh Year and the Jubilee	107
Chapter 13. Sabbath in the Middle	115
A. Daily Sacrifices	116
B. Sabbath Sacrifices	116
C. The Temple	117
Chapter 14. The Early Church and the Feasts	119
Chapter 15. The Significance of the Feast Days	120
Chapter 16. Questions by and for a Seventh-day Adventist Minister	124
Chapter 17. Obedience—Works or Faith?	135
A. The Progressive Nature of the Law	135
B. Biblical Examples of Laodicea	139
Chapter 18. The Sins of Laodicea	141
A. Obedience Declares Faith	145
Chapter 19. The Way Is the Old Way	148
Chapter 20. Rebellion	151
Chapter 21. Summation	160
Chapter 22. Final Warning	164

CHAPTER 1

THE TRUTH

One of the texts all Christians shudder at and move quickly past, saying, "That's not me," is: "And with all deceivableness of unrighteousness in them that perish; because they received not the love of the truth [G225], that they might be saved. And for this cause God shall send them strong delusion, that they should believe a lie: that they all might be damned who believed not the truth [G225], but had pleasure in unrighteousness" (2 Thess. 2:10–12). This text is obviously aimed at Christians at a crucial time in earth's history. It behooves us to know what the Bible defines as truth, that is, as what is true, and see if it matches what we uphold as truth because, unfortunately, many times what passes for truth or what is true is simply the majority opinion on any one issue.

> "
> It behooves us to know what the Bible defines as truth.
> "

Paul, in 2 Thessalonians, is discussing the end of time and the delusion that the evil one has planned for those who have "received not the love of the truth." The delusion is successful amongst those who do not love the truth. So, let us examine ourselves to see if we are one of those who do not love the truth.

The Pharisees and scribes were men who took their religion seriously, and some of them even knew the entirety of the Old Testament Scriptures by heart. However, when God sent His Son, their Creator and Saviour, to live and work among them, they said, "We *know* that this man is a sinner" (John 9:24).

Isaiah spoke of such people, "For the terrible one is brought to nought, and the scorner is consumed, and all that watch ["are on the lookout," H8245] for iniquity are *cut off* [*karath*, H3772]: that make a man an offender for a word, and lay a snare for him that reproveth in the gate, and turn aside the just for a thing of nought" (Isa. 29:20, 21). (In Daniel 9:26, *karath* is the word used in the phrase, "shall Messiah be *cut off*.") These men made *their own "truth"* a test, which Jesus didn't meet, and then judged Him totally by that one test, ignoring the truth He brought them. They became apt examples of a people who, at the end of time, reject God's truth because it doesn't match the paradigm they have chosen. Instead, they choose to poke at, laugh at, and criticize those servants God has sent to invite them to the great celebration that He has planned in His Son's honor.

We will be studying, in this chapter, the texts of the Bible that show what divine truth is. We will include Strong's designation for each term and the definition when it was first used.

"… and *ye shall know the truth* ["true, truly, truth, verity," G225], and the *truth* [G225] *shall make you free*" (John 8:32).

"Behold, thou desirest *truth* ["stability," figuratively "certainty, truth," H571] in the inward parts: and in the hidden part thou shalt make me to know wisdom" (Ps. 51:6).

God's Truth Preserves Us Because It Is Truth

"Have not I written to thee excellent things in counsels and knowledge, that I might make thee know the certainty of the words of *truth* [H571]; that thou mightest answer the words of *truth* [H571] to them that send unto thee?" (Prov. 22:20, 21). *There is certainty in the words of truth.*

"I have not hid thy righteousness within my heart; I have declared thy faithfulness and thy salvation: I have not concealed thy loving kindness and thy *truth* [H571] from the great congregation. Withhold not thou thy tender mercies from me, O LORD: let thy loving kindness and thy *truth* [H571] *continually preserve me*" (Ps. 40:10, 11).

"He shall abide before God for ever: O prepare mercy and *truth* [H571], *which may preserve him*" (Ps. 61:7).

God Is Truth

"He is the Rock, his work is perfect: for all his ways are judgment: *a God of truth* ["firmness, figuratively security, moral fidelity," H530] and without iniquity, just and right is he" (Deut. 32:4).

"But the LORD is the *true* [H571] *God*, he is the living God, and an *everlasting* [H5769] king: at his wrath the earth shall tremble, and the nations shall not be able to abide his indignation" (Jer. 10:10).

Note: The Hebrew word *olam* (H5769), which is translated "forever," "eternity," "vanishing point," "always," and "perpetual" is used here to describe God. It is also used to describe the Sabbath (in Exod. 31:16, 17), to describe the statutes of God (in Lev. 23:14, 21, 31, 41), and to describe all of God's commandments (in Ps. 111:7, 8).

"Into thine hand I commit my spirit: thou hast redeemed me, O LORD *God of truth* [H571]" (Ps. 31:5).

Jesus Is Truth

"Jesus saith unto him, I am the way, the *truth* [G225], and the life: no man cometh unto the Father, but by me" (John 14:6).

"And the Word was made flesh, and dwelt among us, (and we beheld his glory, the glory as of the only begotten of the Father,) *full of grace and truth*" (John 1:14). Jesus was full of grace and *truth* [G225].

"For the law was given by Moses, but grace and *truth* [G225] *came by Jesus Christ*" (John 1:17).

God's Words Are Truth

"Thy word is *true* [H571] from the beginning: and every one of thy righteous judgments endureth *for ever* ["everlasting," H5769]" (Ps. 119:160).

"Sanctify them through thy truth [G225]: thy word is truth [G225]" (John 17:17).

"And now, O Lord GOD, thou art that God, and *thy words be true* [H571], and thou hast promised this goodness unto thy servant" (2 Sam. 7:28).

Scripture Is Truth

"But I will shew thee that which is noted in the *scripture of truth* [H571]: and there is none that holdeth with me in these things, but Michael your prince" (Dan. 10:21).

The Gospel Is the Truth

[Christ] "In whom ye also trusted, after that ye heard the word of *truth* [G225], *the gospel of your salvation*: in whom also after that ye believed, ye were sealed with that holy Spirit of promise" (Eph. 1:13).

"To whom we gave place by subjection, no, not for an hour; that the *truth* [G225] *of the gospel* might continue with you" (Gal. 2:5).

"Study to shew thyself approved unto God, a workman that needeth not to be ashamed, rightly dividing the *word of truth* [G225]" (2 Tim. 2:15).

"And the servant of the Lord must not strive; but be gentle unto all men, apt to teach, patient, in meekness *instructing those that oppose themselves*; if God peradventure will give them repentance to the acknowledging *of the truth* [G225]" (2 Tim. 2:24, 25).

God's Commandments are Truth

"The works of his hands are verity [H571] and judgment; *all* his commandments are sure. They stand fast for *ever* ["perpetual," H5703] and *ever* ["everlasting," H5769], and are done in *truth* [H571] and uprightness" (Ps. 111:7, 8).

The *Torah* Is Truth

"Thy righteousness is an everlasting righteousness, and thy *law* [torah, H8451] *is the truth* [H571]" (Ps. 119:142).

"Thou camest down also upon mount Sinai, and spakest with them from heaven, and gavest them right *judgments*, and *true* [H571] *laws* [torah, H8451], good *statutes* [H2706] and *commandments* [H4687]" (Neh. 9:13).

> "Thy righteousness is an everlasting righteousness, and thy law [torah, H8451] is the truth [H571]" (Ps. 119:142).

"The *law* [torah, H8451] of *truth* [H571] was in his mouth, and iniquity was not found in his lips: he walked with me in peace and equity, and did turn many away from iniquity. For the priest's lips should keep knowledge, and they should seek the *law* [torah, H8451] at his mouth: for he is the messenger of the LORD of hosts. But ye are departed out of the way; ye have caused many to stumble at the *law* [torah, H8451]; ye have corrupted the covenant of Levi, saith the LORD of hosts. Therefore have I also made you contemptible and base before all the people, according as ye have not kept my ways, but have been *partial in the law* [torah, H8451]" (Mal. 2:6–9).

The *Torah* Is the Arbiter of Truth

"To the *law* [*torah*, H8451] and the *testimony* ["attestation," H8584]: if they speak not according to this word, it is because there is no light in them" (Isa. 8:20).

"Thy righteousness is an everlasting righteousness, and thy *law* [*torah*, H8451] *is the truth* [H571]" (Ps. 119:142).

"As it is written in the *law* [*torah*, H8451] of Moses, all this evil is come upon us: yet made we not our prayer before the LORD our God, that we might turn from *our iniquities* ["perversity, moral evil, sin," H5771], and understand thy *truth* [H571]" (Dan. 9:13).

The *Torah* and the Judgments of God Are Arbiters of Truth

"The *law* [*torah*, H8451] of the LORD *is perfect, converting the soul*: the *testimony of the LORD is sure*, making wise the simple. The *statutes of the LORD are right, rejoicing* the heart: *the commandment of the LORD is pure*, enlightening the eyes. The *fear of the LORD is* clean, *enduring* for *ever* ["everlasting," H5703]: the judgments of the LORD are *true* [H571] and righteous altogether" (Ps. 19:7–9).

Note: All of the above gifts of God are for our salvation and happiness, and the word translated "testimony" (H5715) is the same word used to the describe the ark of the testimony.

"I have chosen the way of *truth* [H530]: thy judgments have I laid before me" (Ps. 119:30).

"... the soul that sinneth, it shall die. But if a man be just, and do that which is *lawful* and *right*, and hath not eaten upon the mountains, neither hath lifted up his eyes to the idols of the house of Israel, neither hath defiled his neighbour's wife, neither hath come near to a menstruous woman, and hath not oppressed any, but hath restored to the debtor his pledge, hath spoiled none by violence, hath given his bread to the hungry, and hath covered the naked with a garment; he that hath not given forth upon *usury*, neither hath taken any increase, that hath withdrawn his hand from iniquity, hath executed *true* [H571] judgment between man and man, hath *walked in my statutes*, and *hath kept my judgments*, to deal *truly* [H571]; he is just, *he shall surely live*, saith the Lord GOD" (Ezek. 18:4–9).

"And the word of the LORD came unto Zechariah, saying, Thus speaketh the LORD of hosts, saying, Execute *true* [H571] judgment, and shew mercy and compassions every man to his brother: and oppress not the widow, nor the fatherless, the stranger, nor the poor; and let none of you imagine evil against his brother in your heart. *But they refused to hearken, and pulled away the shoulder, and stopped their ears, that they should not hear.* Yea, they made their hearts as an adamant stone, lest they should hear the law [*torah*, H8451], and the words which the LORD of hosts hath sent in his spirit by the former prophets: therefore came a great wrath from the LORD of hosts" (Zech. 7:8–12).

Note: The teachings of Jesus, in the two texts above, are true, right, and pure. Notice also that even the activities associated with idol worship—the festal gatherings where they ate upon the mountain—were forbidden.

Why is God so particular? It is because we are His children. He made us, redeemed us, and saved us. He knows what will draw us to Him and what will pull us away from Him. We see, in one of the above texts, what and how God's people in Zechariah's time received truth. Let's look at a few more.

"And testifiedst against them, that thou mightest bring them again unto thy *law* [*torah*, H8451]: yet they dealt proudly, and hearkened not unto thy commandments, but sinned against thy judgments, (which if a man do, he shall live in them;) and withdrew the shoulder, and hardened their neck, and would not hear" (Neh. 9:29).

"But it shall come to pass, if thou wilt not hearken unto the voice of the LORD thy God, to observe to do *all his commandments and his statutes* which I command thee this day; that all these curses shall come upon thee, and overtake thee: ... Turn ye from your evil ways, and *keep my commandments and my statutes*, according to *all the law* [*torah*, H8451] which I commanded your fathers, and which I sent to you by my servants the prophets. Notwithstanding they would not hear, but hardened their necks, like to the neck of their fathers, that did not believe in the LORD their God. And they *rejected his statutes*, and *his covenant* [H1285] that he made with their fathers, and his testimonies which he testified against them; and they followed vanity, and became vain, and went after the heathen that were round about them, concerning whom the LORD had charged them, that they should not do like them" (Deut. 28:15; 2 Kings 17:13–15).

What does God say will occur in the future?

"And they shall turn away their ears from the truth [G225], and shall be turned unto fables" (2 Tim. 4:4).

Laodicea is told to buy gold, *symbolic of* Christ's righteousness. What else should we buy? "Buy the truth [H571], and sell it not ..." (Prov. 23:23).

Why is truth essential to Laodicea? "Before the LORD: for he cometh, for he cometh to the earth: he shall judge the world with righteousness, and the people with his *truth* [H530]" (Ps. 96:13).

Let's go back to our opening text, 2 Thessalonians 2:10–12. What is the truth that the people at the end of time don't love or receive? The answer regarding truth is noted in verse 7. "For the mystery of *iniquity* ["lawlessness," G458] doth already work: only he who now letteth will let, until he be taken out of the way" (2 Thess. 2:7). The truth that is not loved at the end of time is God's *law*. "And then will I profess unto them, I never knew you: depart from me, ye that work *iniquity* ["lawlessness," G458]" (Matt. 7:23).

Why Truth Is Not Loved

"But this thing commanded I them, saying, Obey my voice, and I will be your God, and ye shall be my people: and walk ye in all the ways that I have commanded you, that it may be well unto you. But they *hearkened not, nor inclined their ear*, but walked in the counsels ["purposes," H4156] and in the *imagination* ["stubbornness," H8307] of their evil heart, and went backward, and not forward" (Jer. 7:23, 24).

"And the LORD saith, Because they have forsaken my law [H8451] which I set before them, and have not obeyed my voice, neither walked therein; but have walked after the *imagination* ["stubbornness," H8307] of their own heart, and after Baalim, which their fathers taught them" (Jer. 9:13, 14).

"For I earnestly protested unto your fathers in the day that I brought them up out of the land of Egypt, even unto this day, rising early and protesting, saying, Obey my voice. Yet they obeyed not, nor inclined their ear, but walked every one in the *imagination* ["stubbornness," H8307] of their evil heart: therefore I will bring upon them all the words of this *covenant* [H1285], which I commanded them to do: but they did them not" (Jer. 11:7, 8; see Deut. 28:1–29:1).

Note: Jeremiah and Moses describe God's chosen people's response to the promptings by His messages as walking in the *imagination* ["stubbornness," H8307] of their own heart. God, through the prophet Samuel, tells us: "For rebellion is as the sin of witchcraft and *stubbornness* is as iniquity and *idolatry*." Any paradigm we choose over the counsel of God in the Scriptures is the same as idol worship. This is why the Jews rejected Jesus and why we are at risk at the end of time.

"This know also, that in the last days perilous times shall come. For men shall be lovers of their own selves, covetous, boasters, proud, blasphemers, disobedient to parents, *unthankful*, unholy, ... ever learning, and never able to come to the *knowledge of the truth* [G225]. Now as Jannes and Jambres withstood Moses, *so do these also resist the truth* [G225]: men of corrupt minds, reprobate concerning the *faith* ["conviction of religious truth," G4102]" (2 Tim. 3:1, 2, 7, 8).

"But your iniquities have separated between you and your God, and your sins have hid his face from you, that he will not hear. None calleth for justice, nor any pleadeth for *truth* [H530]: they trust in vanity, and speak lies; they conceive mischief, and bring forth iniquity. Therefore is judgment far from us, neither doth justice overtake us: we wait for light, but behold obscurity; for brightness, but we walk in darkness. We grope for the wall *like the blind*, and we grope *as if we had no eyes: we stumble at noon day as in the night*; we are in desolate places as dead men. In transgressing and lying against the LORD, and departing away from our God, speaking oppression and revolt, conceiving and uttering from the heart words of *falsehood* ["an untruth," H8267]. And judgment is turned away backward, and justice standeth afar off: for *truth* [H571] is fallen in the street, and equity cannot enter. Yea, *truth* [H571] faileth; and he that departeth from evil maketh himself a prey: and the LORD saw it, and it displeased him that there was no judgment" (Isa. 59:2, 4, 9, 10, 13–15).

"But my people would not hearken to my voice; and Israel would none of me. So I gave them up unto their own hearts' *lust* ["stubbornness," H8307]: and they walked in their own counsels. Oh that my people had hearkened unto me, and Israel had walked in my ways! The haters of the LORD should have submitted themselves unto him: but their time should have endured for *ever* ["everlasting," H5769]" (Ps. 81:11–13, 15).

Where Truth Is Found

"This principle we in our day are firmly to maintain. The banner of truth and religious liberty held aloft by the founders of the gospel church and by God's witnesses during the centuries that have passed since then, has, in this last conflict, been committed to our hands. The responsibility for this great gift rests with those whom God has blessed with a knowledge of His word. We are to receive this word as supreme authority. God's word must be recognized as above all human legislation. A *'Thus saith the Lord'* is not to be set aside for a *'Thus saith the church'* or a *'Thus saith the state'*" (AA 68.2).

"But God will have a people upon the earth to maintain the Bible, and the Bible only, as the *standard of all doctrines* and the *basis of all reforms*. The opinions of learned men, the deductions of science, the *creeds* or decisions of ecclesiastical councils, as numerous and discordant as are the churches which they represent, the voice of the majority—not one nor all of these should be regarded as evidence for or against any point of religious faith. Before accepting any doctrine or precept, we should demand a plain *'Thus saith the Lord'* in its support" (GC 595.1).

"Though the Reformation gave the Scriptures to all, yet the selfsame principle which was maintained by Rome prevents multitudes in Protestant churches from searching the Bible for themselves. They are taught to accept its teachings as *interpreted by the church*; and there are thousands who dare receive nothing, however plainly revealed in Scripture, that is contrary to their *creed* or *the established teaching of their church*" (GC 596.3).

"In His word, God has committed to men the knowledge necessary for salvation. The Holy Scriptures are to be accepted as an *authoritative, infallible revelation* of His will. They are the *standard of character*, the *revealer of doctrines*, and the *test of experience*. 'Every scripture inspired of God is also profitable for teaching, for reproof, for correction, for instruction which is in righteousness; that the man of God may be complete, furnished completely unto every good work.' 2 Timothy 3:16, 17, Revised Version" (GC vii.1).

Our testimony must be: "We dare not tamper with God's word, dividing His holy law; *calling one portion essential and another nonessential*, to gain the favor of the world" (GC 610.1).

"With the issue thus clearly brought before him, whoever shall trample upon *God's law* to obey a *human enactment* receives the mark of the beast; he accepts the sign of allegiance to the power which he chooses to obey instead of God" (GC 604.3).

Jesus said, "Think not that I am come to destroy the law, or the prophets: I am not come to destroy, but to fulfil ["to complete," G4137]. For verily I say unto you, Till heaven and earth pass, one jot or one tittle shall in no wise pass from the law, till all be fulfilled. *Whosoever therefore shall break one of these least commandments*, and shall teach men so, *he shall be called the least in the kingdom of heaven*: but whosoever shall do and teach them, the same shall be called great in the kingdom of heaven" (Matt. 5:17–19).

"The testimony of the word of God is against this ensnaring doctrine of faith without works. *It is not faith that claims the favor of Heaven without complying with the conditions upon which mercy is to be granted, it is presumption*; for genuine faith has its foundation in the promises and provisions of the Scriptures. Let none deceive themselves with the belief that they can become holy while *willfully violating one of God's requirements*. The commission of a known sin silences the witnessing voice of the Spirit and *separates the soul from God*. 'Sin is the transgression of the law.' And 'whosoever sinneth ["transgresseth the law"] hath not seen Him, neither known Him.' 1 John 3:6. Though John in his epistles dwells so fully upon love, yet he does not hesitate to reveal the true character of that class who claim to be sanctified while living in transgression of the law of God. '*He that saith, I know Him, and keepeth not His commandments, is a liar, and the truth is not in him. But whoso keepeth His word, in him verily is the love of God perfected*.' 1 John 2:4, 5. Here is the test of every man's profession. We cannot accord holiness to any man without bringing him to the measurement of God's only standard of holiness in heaven and in earth. If men feel no weight of the *moral law*, if they belittle and make light of God's *precepts*, if they break *one of the least of these commandments*, and teach men so, they shall be of no esteem in the sight of Heaven, and we may know that their claims are without foundation" (GC 472.2, 3).

Those who are living upon the earth when the intercession of Christ shall cease in the sanctuary above are to stand in the sight of a holy God without a mediator. Their robes must be spotless, their characters must be purified from sin by the *blood of sprinkling. Through the grace of God* and *their own diligent effort* they must be conquerors in the battle with evil. While the investigative judgment is going forward in heaven, while the sins of penitent believers are being removed from the sanctuary, there is to be a special work of purification, of putting away of sin, among God's people upon earth. This work is more clearly presented in the messages of Revelation 14.

"When this work shall have been accomplished, the followers of Christ will be ready for His appearing. 'Then shall the offering of Judah and Jerusalem be pleasant unto the Lord, as in the days of old, and as in former years.' Malachi 3:4. Then the church which our Lord at His coming is to receive to Himself will be a 'glorious church, not having spot, or wrinkle, or any such thing.' Ephesians 5:27. Then she will look 'forth as the morning, fair as the moon, clear as the sun, and terrible as an army with banners.' Song of Solomon 6:10" (GC 425.1, 2, emphasis added)

We continue in God's grace and, through the Holy Spirit's power, are able to overcome sin!

CHAPTER 2

THE LAW AND SALVATION

For a while, shortly after the Creation, there was a time when the man and his wife enjoyed a right relationship with God. There will be a time again before Jesus returns when God's children are again in the right relationship with their Father. Healthy, happy, obedient and submissive to God's law, Adam and his wife were never under the law. They loved their Creator and strove to please Him. Jesus said, "Howbeit when he, the Spirit of *truth* [G225], is come, he will guide you into all truth: for he shall not speak of himself; but whatsoever he shall hear, that shall he speak: and he will shew you things to come. He shall glorify me: for he shall receive of mine, and shall shew it unto you" (John 16:13, 14). So, what does Scripture say? And into what *truth* [G225] will He guide us? "And when he is come, he will reprove the world of sin, and of righteousness, and of judgment" (John 16:8). The Holy Spirit reveals *God's law, showing sins, Christ and obedience to the law, showing righteousness; or rejection of the Saviour and the law, showing judgment*. "And that ye put on the new man, which after God is created in righteousness and true holiness" (Eph. 4:24).

There are three gifts from God that make our salvation possible.

> "For a while, shortly after the Creation, there was a time when the man and his wife enjoyed a right relationship with God. There will be a time again before Jesus returns when God's children are again in the right relationship with their Father."

Grace

"For by grace are ye saved through faith; and that not of yourselves: it is the gift of God" (Eph. 2:8).

"But unto every one of us is given grace according to the measure of the gift of Christ" (Eph. 4:7).

"And the grace of our Lord was exceeding abundant with faith and love which is in Christ Jesus" (1 Tim. 1:14).

"But Noah found grace in the eyes of the LORD" (Gen. 6:8).

"And now for a little space grace hath been shewed from the LORD our God, to leave us a remnant to escape, and to give us a nail in his holy place, that our God may lighten our eyes, and give us a little reviving in our bondage" (Ezra 9:8).

Faith

"For by grace are ye saved through faith; and that not of yourselves: it is the gift of God" (Eph. 2:8).

"For therein is the righteousness of God revealed from faith to faith: as it is written, The just shall live by faith" (Rom. 1:17).

"Behold, his soul which is lifted up is not upright in him: but the just shall live by his faith" (Hab. 2:4).

"And they rose early in the morning, and went forth into the wilderness of Tekoa: and as they went forth, Jehoshaphat stood and said, Hear me, O Judah, and ye inhabitants of Jerusalem; believe in the LORD your God, so shall ye be established; believe his prophets, so shall ye prosper" (2 Chron. 20:20).

The Sacrifice of Christ

"Pilate therefore said unto him, Art thou a king then? Jesus answered, Thou sayest that I am a king. To this end was I born, and for this cause came I into the world, that I should bear witness unto the truth [G225]. Every one that is of the truth [G225] heareth my voice" (John 18:37).

Paul says, in Hebrews 9:22, that, without the shedding of blood, there is no remission.

"But this man, after he had offered one sacrifice for sins for ever, sat down on the right hand of God" (Heb. 10:12).

The Law and Salvation

The sacrifice of Christ was made necessary by man's relationship to the law. After sin, God asked Job, "Knowest thou the ordinances ["statutes," H2708] *of heaven*? canst thou set the dominion ["jurisdiction," H4896] thereof in the earth?" (Job 38:33). In other words, the laws that govern heaven have to do with the jurisdiction or the official power to make legal decisions in the earth.

"He [Lucifer] began to insinuate doubts concerning the *laws that governed heavenly beings*, intimating that though laws might be necessary for the inhabitants of the worlds, angels, being more exalted, needed no such restraint, for their own wisdom was a sufficient guide" (PP 37.1).

"Lucifer was convinced that he was in the wrong. He [Lucifer] saw that 'the Lord is righteous in all His ways, and holy in all His works' (Ps. 145:17); that the *divine statutes* are just, and that he ought to acknowledge them as such before all heaven" (PP 39.1).

"He [Satan] denounced the *divine statutes* as a restriction of their liberty and declared that it was his purpose to secure the abolition of law; that, freed from this restraint, the hosts of heaven might enter upon a more exalted, more glorious state of existence" (GC 499.2).

So, what are those statutes that govern heaven and that Lucifer hated?

"Ezra became a mouthpiece for God, educating those about him in the principles that *govern heaven*" (PK 609.2).

"This Ezra went up from Babylon; and he was a ready scribe in the law of Moses, which the LORD God of Israel had given: and the king granted him all his request, according to the hand of the LORD his God upon him. For Ezra had prepared his heart *to seek the law of the LORD*, and to do it, and to teach in Israel *statutes* and *judgments*" (Ezra 7:6, 10).

"More than two thousand years have passed since Ezra 'prepared his heart to seek the law [*torah*] of the Lord, and to do it' (Ezra 7:10), yet the lapse of time has not lessened the influence of his pious example. Through the centuries the record of his life of consecration has inspired many with the determination 'to seek the law of the Lord, and to do it.'

"In this age of the world, when Satan is seeking, through manifold agencies, to blind the eyes of men and women to the *binding claims of the law of God*, there is need of men who can cause many to 'tremble at the commandment of our God.' Ezra 10:3. There is need of true reformers, who will point transgressors to the great Lawgiver and teach them that 'the law [*torah*] of the Lord is perfect, converting the soul' (Ps. 19:7). There is need of men mighty in the Scriptures, men whose every word and act exalts the *statutes* of Jehovah, men who seek to strengthen faith.

Teachers are needed, oh, so much, who will inspire hearts with reverence and love for the Scriptures" (PK 623.4).

"In the *truths* of His word, God has given to men a revelation of Himself; and to all who accept them they are a shield against the deceptions of Satan. It is a neglect of these truths that has opened the door to the evils which are now becoming so widespread in the religious world. The *nature* and the *importance* of the law of God have been, to a great extent, lost sight of. A wrong *conception* of the *character*, the *perpetuity*, and the *obligation* of the divine law has led to errors in relation to conversion and sanctification, and has resulted in lowering the standard of piety in the church. Here is to be found the secret of the lack of the Spirit and power of God in the revivals of our time.

" '*One source of danger is the neglect of the pulpit to enforce the divine law*. In former days the pulpit was an echo of the voice of conscience. ... Our most illustrious preachers gave a wonderful majesty to their discourses by following the example of the Master, and giving prominence to the law, its precepts, and its threatenings. They repeated the *two great maxims*, that *the law is a transcript of the divine perfections*, and that *a man who does not love the law does not love the gospel*; for *the law, as well as the gospel, is a mirror reflecting the true character of God*. This peril leads to another, that of underrating the evil of sin, the extent of it, the demerit of it. In proportion to the rightfulness of the commandment is the wrongfulness of disobeying it....' " (GC 465.2).

Jesus said that obedience to the law, both the big and little commandments, was required for salvation: "Whosoever therefore shall break one of these least commandments, and shall teach men so, he shall be called the least in the kingdom of heaven: but whosoever shall do and teach them, the same shall be called great in the kingdom of heaven" (Matt. 5:19).

"Thou knowest the commandments, Do not commit adultery, Do not kill, Do not steal, Do not bear false witness, *Defraud not*, Honour thy father and mother. And he answered and said unto him, Master, all these have I observed from my youth. Then Jesus beholding him loved him, and said unto him, One thing thou lackest: go thy way, sell whatsoever thou hast, and give to the poor, and thou shalt have treasure in heaven: and come, take up the cross, and follow me" (Mark 10:19–21).

Note: Jesus included the statute found in Leviticus 19:13, regarding defrauding your neighbor.

"Honour thy father and thy mother: and, *Thou shalt love thy neighbour as thyself.* The young man saith unto him, All these things have I kept from my youth up: what lack I yet? Jesus said unto him, If thou wilt be perfect, go and sell that thou hast, and give to the poor, and thou shalt have treasure in heaven: and come and follow me" (Matt. 19:19–21).

Note: In this text, Jesus includes a foundational statement from the law of Moses found in Leviticus 19:18.

"God has given us His word that we may become acquainted with its teachings and know for ourselves what He requires of us. When the lawyer came to Jesus with the inquiry, 'What shall I do to inherit eternal life?' the Saviour referred him to the Scriptures, saying: 'What is written in the law? how readest thou?' [Luke 10:26.] *Ignorance will not excuse young or old, nor release them from the punishment due for the transgression of God's law*; because there *is in their hands a faithful presentation of that law* and of its principles and claims. *It is not enough* to have *good intentions*; it is not enough *to do what a man thinks is right or what the minister tells him is right*. His soul's salvation is at stake, and *he should search the Scriptures for himself*. However strong may be his convictions, however confident he may be that the minister knows what is truth, this is not his foundation. He has a chart pointing out every waymark on the heavenward journey, and he ought not to guess at anything" (GC 598.1).

"The teaching which has become so widespread, that the divine *statutes* are no longer binding upon men, is the same as *idolatry* in its effect upon the morals of the people. Those who seek to lessen the claims of God's holy law are striking directly at the *foundation* of the government of families and nations. Religious parents, failing to walk in His *statutes*, do not command their household to keep the way of the Lord. The *law* of God is not made the rule of life. The children, as they make homes of their own, feel under no obligation to teach their children what they themselves have never been taught. And this is why there are so many godless families; this is why depravity is so deep and widespread" (PP 143.1).

"*The sacred statutes* which Satan has hated and sought to destroy, will be honored throughout a sinless universe. And 'as the earth bringeth forth her bud, and as the garden causeth the things that are sown in it to spring forth; so the Lord God will cause righteousness and praise to spring forth before all nations.' Isaiah 61:11" (PP 342.2).

What is the difference between not obeying well and rebellion? Not obeying well, not meeting the mark of perfection demanded by God, *requires the grace of God*. Rebellion states, "I don't have to do that!" *Rebellion doesn't need grace*! Rebellion doesn't even try. Rebellion states that there is no law or that the law was *done away with*. "Wherefore doth the wicked contemn ["despise," H5006] God? he hath said in his heart, Thou wilt not require it" (Ps. 10:13).

When we dispute with God regarding the statutes that govern heaven, we are attacking the foundation of God's government, His very being, and His right to be God!

Grace requires submission to the law of God. Rebellion doesn't know what submission is. To understand grace is to realize how far short of God's requirements we fall and how sin has separated us from our Father. But, it also gives us hope that He will accept us if we return and follow His ways.

> "
> When we dispute with God regarding the statutes that govern heaven, we are attacking the foundation of God's government, His very being, and His right to be God!
> "

Note: In Exodus 20:6, God tells us that He shows mercy to those who love Him and keep His commandments. Mercy is the grace we need to stand before God through the faith He gives us.

"In the beginning, God gave His law to mankind as a means of *attaining happiness* and eternal life. Satan's only hope of thwarting the purpose of God is to lead men and women to disobey this law, and his constant effort has been to misrepresent its teachings and belittle its importance. His master stroke has been an attempt to change the law itself, so as to lead men *to violate its precepts* while *professing to obey it*" (PK 178.2).

Joshua said, "But take diligent heed to do the commandment *and the law* [*torah*, H8451], which Moses the servant of the LORD charged you, to love the LORD your God, and to walk in all his ways, and to keep his commandments, and to cleave unto him, and to serve him with all your heart and with all your soul" (Joshua 22:5).

Leadership and the Law

Regarding our leaders, God said, "Come up to me into the mount, and be there: and I will give thee tables of stone, *and a law* [*torah*, H8451], and commandments which I have written; that thou mayest teach them" (Exod. 24:12).

Regarding the king, Moses said, "And it [the *Torah*] shall be with him, and he shall read therein all the days of his life: that he may learn to fear the LORD his God, to keep all the words of this law [*torah*, H8451] *and these statutes*, to do them" (Deut. 17:19).

The following texts reveal that God has not changed His mind about His law.

"By this we know that we love the children of God, when we love God, and keep his commandments. For this is the love of God, that we keep his commandments: and his commandments are not grievous" (1 John 5:2, 3).

This message to the early church reflects what Moses said: *"For this commandment which I command you today is not too difficult for you, nor is it out of reach"* (Deut. 30:11, New American Standard Bible, 1995).

The Spirit and the Law

If we are led by the Spirit, do we need the law?

"And this is his commandment, That we should believe on the name of his Son Jesus Christ, and love one another, as he gave us commandment. And he that keepeth his commandments dwelleth in him, and he in him. And hereby we know that he abideth in us, by the Spirit which he hath given us" (1 John 3:23, 24).

"For what the law could not do, in that it was weak through the flesh, God sending his own Son in the likeness of sinful flesh, and for sin, condemned sin in the flesh: that the righteousness of the law might be fulfilled in us, who walk not after the flesh, but after the Spirit. For they that are after the flesh do mind the things of the flesh; but they that are after the Spirit the things of the Spirit. For to be carnally minded is death; but to be spiritually minded is life and peace. Because the carnal mind is enmity against God: *for it is not subject to the law of God*, neither indeed can be. So then they that are in the flesh cannot please God" (Rom. 8:3–8).

Regarding the Holy Spirit and the law, Jesus said, "Nevertheless I tell you the *truth* [G225]; it is expedient for you that I go away: for if I go not away, the Comforter will not come unto you; but if I depart, I will send him unto you. And when he is come, he will reprove the world of *sin*, and of *righteousness*, and of *judgment*" (John 16:7, 8). *Sin* is the transgression of *the law*. *Righteousness* is the keeping of *the law*. *The law* is what we will be judged by, if we are not submissive to Christ and *His law*.

Coming to Christ

"We build on Christ by obeying His word. It is not he who merely enjoys righteousness that is righteous, but he who does righteousness. Holiness is not rapture; *it is the result of surrendering all to God; it is doing the will of our heavenly Father*. When the children of Israel were encamped on the borders of the Promised Land, it was not enough for them to have a knowledge of Canaan, or to sing the songs of Canaan. This alone would not bring them into possession of the vineyards and olive groves of the goodly land. They could make it theirs in truth only by occupation, by complying with the conditions, by exercising living faith in God, by appropriating His promises to themselves, *while they obeyed His instruction*.

"*Religion consists in doing the words of Christ*; not doing to earn God's favor, but because, all undeserving, we have received the gift of His love. Christ places the salvation of man, not upon profession merely, *but upon faith that is made manifest in works of righteousness*. Doing, not saying merely, is expected of the followers of Christ. It is through action that character is built. '*As many as are led by the Spirit of God, they are the sons of God.*' Romans 8:14. Not those whose hearts are touched by the Spirit, not those who now and then yield to its power, but *they that are led by the Spirit, are the sons of God*.

"Do you desire to become a follower of Christ, yet know not how to begin? Are you in darkness and know not how to find the light? *Follow the light you have. Set your heart to obey what you do know of the word of God. His power, His very life, dwells in His word. As you receive the word in faith, it will give you power to obey*. As you give heed to the light you have, greater light will come. You are building on God's word, and your character will be builded after the similitude of the character of Christ" (MB 150.1).

Ellen White wrote, concerning Christ: "None but Christ can fashion anew the character that has been ruined by sin. He came to expel the demons that had controlled the will. He came to lift us up from the dust, to reshape the marred character after the pattern of His divine character, and to make it beautiful with His own glory" (DA 37.3).

Putting It All Together

Jesus said that He did not come to destroy the law or the prophets. "Think not that I am come to destroy the law, or the prophets: I am not come to destroy, but to fulfil" (Matt. 5:17). A lawyer asked, "Master, what shall I do to inherit eternal life?" (Luke 10:25). Here are two questions from the mind of Christ regarding our salvation that Jesus answered the lawyer with: *"What is written in the law? How readest thou?"* (Luke 10:26).

The lawyer's answer, in Deuteronomy 6:1–5 and Leviticus 19:18, was from the "law of Moses."

"Now these are the *commandments*, the *statutes*, and the *judgments*, which the LORD your God commanded to teach you, that ye might do them in the land whither ye go to possess it: that thou mightest fear the LORD thy God, to keep all his *statutes and* his *commandments*, which I command thee, thou, and thy son, and thy son's son, all the days of thy life; and that thy days may be prolonged. Hear therefore, O Israel, and observe to do it; that it may be well with thee, and that ye may increase mightily, as the LORD God of thy fathers hath promised thee, in the land that floweth with milk and honey. Hear, O Israel: the LORD our God is one LORD: and thou shalt *love the LORD thy God with all thine heart, and with all thy soul, and with all thy might*" (Deut. 6:1–5).

"Thou shalt not avenge, nor bear any grudge against the children of thy people, but thou shalt *love thy neighbour as thyself*: I am the LORD" (Lev. 19:18).

Now Christ answered, "And he said unto him, Thou hast answered right: this do, and thou shalt live" (Luke 10:28). Notice, Jesus praised the lawyer for ferreting out the two basic premises of *all law, both of which are the basis of the relationship between God and man*. Grace and faith are also aspects of our relationships with God and each other. In establishing a relationship or re-establishing a relationship, *love* is the root of both. Jesus said, "If ye love me, keep my commandments" (John 14:15).

Pay attention! Jesus said, "And if any man hear my words, and believe not, I judge him not: for I came not to judge the world, but to save the world. He that rejecteth me, and receiveth not my words, hath one that judgeth him: *the word that I have spoken, the same shall judge him in the last day*" (John 12:47, 48).

With what did Jesus *equate His words* that we are to be judged by? Jesus said, "For had ye believed Moses, ye would have believed me; for he wrote of me. But if ye believe not *his writings*, how shall ye believe my words?" (John 5:46, 47).

These texts are a fulfillment of a prophecy in Deuteronomy.

"I will raise them up a Prophet from among their brethren, *like unto thee*, and will put my words in his mouth; and he shall speak unto them all that I shall command him. And it shall come to pass, *that whosoever will not hearken unto my words which he shall speak in my name, I will require it of him*" (Deut. 18:18, 19).

CHAPTER 3

THE LAW OF MOSES

"They cast aside the restraint of the law, and give loose rein to the corrupt passions and the promptings of the natural heart, and then triumph in the mercy and grace of the gospel. Christ speaks to such: 'Not every one that saith unto me, Lord, Lord, shall enter into the kingdom of Heaven; but he that doeth the will of my Father which is in Heaven.' What is the will of the Father? That we keep his commandments. Christ, to enforce the will of his Father, became the author of the statutes and precepts given through Moses to the people of God. Christians who extol Christ, but array themselves against the law governing the Jewish church, array Christ against Christ" (*Review and Herald*, May 6, 1875, par. 16).

"The principles set forth in Deuteronomy for the instruction of Israel are to be followed by God's people to the end of time" (PK 570.2).

"*Moses of himself framed no law*. Christ, the angel whom God had appointed to go before his chosen people, gave to Moses statutes and requirements necessary to a living religion and to govern the people of God. Christians commit a terrible mistake in calling this law severe and arbitrary, and then contrasting it with the gospel and mission of Christ in his ministry on earth, as though he were in opposition to the just precepts which they call the law of Moses" (*Review and Herald*, May 6, 1875, par. 12).

Are the people of God today any different from the people of God in Moses' day? No! More importantly, is the God of the people in Moses' day any different from the God of the people today? No! Neither are His requirements! "For I am the Lord, I change not …" (Mal. 3:6).

"God has placed in His word no command which men may obey or disobey at will and not suffer the consequences. If men choose any other path than that of strict obedience, they will find that 'the end thereof are the ways of death.' Proverbs 14:12" (PP 360.2).

"There must be no withholding on our part, of our service or our means, if we would fulfil our covenant with God. 'This day the Lord thy God hath commanded thee to do these statutes and judgments: thou shalt therefore keep and do them with all thine heart, and with all thy soul.' [Deuteronomy 26:16.] The purpose of all God's commandments is to reveal man's duty not only to God, but to his fellow man. In this late age of the world's history, we are not, because of the selfishness of our hearts, to question or dispute the *right of God to make these requirements*, or we will deceive ourselves and rob our souls of the richest blessings of the grace of God. Heart and mind and soul are to be merged in the will of God. *Then the covenant, framed by the dictates of infinite wisdom, and made binding by the power and authority of the King of kings and Lord of lords, will be our pleasure. God will have no controversy with us in regard to these binding precepts. It is enough that He has said that obedience to His statutes and laws is the life and prosperity of His people*" (Ms. 67, 1907, par. 10).

"True faith, which relies wholly upon Christ, will be manifested by obedience to all the requirements of God. From Adam's day to the present time the great controversy has been concerning obedience to God's law. In all ages there have been those who claimed a right to the favor of God even while they were disregarding *some* of His commands. But the Scriptures declare that by works is 'faith made perfect;' and that, without the works of obedience, faith 'is dead.' James 2:22, 17. He that professes to know God, 'and keepeth not His commandments, is a liar, and the truth is not in him.' 1 John 2:4" (PP 73.2).

The Ceremonial Law

What was Nailed to the Cross?

"Then, said the angel, 'He shall confirm the covenant with many for one week [seven years].' For seven years after the Saviour entered on His ministry, the gospel was to be preached especially to the Jews; for three and a half years by Christ Himself, and afterward by the apostles. 'In the midst of the week He shall cause the sacrifice and the oblation to cease.' Daniel 9:27. In the spring of A.D. 31, Christ, the true Sacrifice, was offered on Calvary. Then the veil of the temple was rent in twain, showing that the sacredness and significance of the sacrificial service had departed. The time had come for the *earthly sacrifice* and *oblation to cease*" (PK 699.1).

Paul, in Hebrews 9:1–28, tells us of the earthly sanctuary services and how the death of our Saviour fulfilled the sacrificial requirements involved with the temple services here on earth.

"Now when these things were thus ordained, the priests went always into the first tabernacle, accomplishing the service of God. But into the second went the high priest alone once every year, *not without blood*, which he offered for himself, and for the errors of the people: the Holy Ghost this signifying, that the way into the holiest of all was not yet made manifest, while as the first tabernacle was yet standing: which was a figure for the time then present, in which were offered both gifts and sacrifices, that could not make him that did the service perfect, as pertaining to the conscience; which stood only in meats and drinks, and divers washings, and carnal ordinances, imposed on them until the time of reformation. But Christ being come an high priest of good things to come, by a greater and more perfect tabernacle, not made with hands, that is to say, not of this building; neither by the blood of goats and calves, but by his own blood he entered in once into the holy place, having obtained eternal redemption for us. For if the blood of bulls and of goats, and the ashes of an heifer sprinkling the unclean, sanctifieth to the purifying of the flesh: how much more shall the blood of Christ, who through the eternal Spirit offered himself without spot to God, purge your conscience from dead works to serve the living God? *And almost all things are by the law purged with blood; and without shedding of blood is no remission*" (Heb. 9:6–14, 22).

"Through long intercourse with idolaters the people of Israel had mingled many heathen customs with their worship; therefore the Lord gave them at Sinai definite instruction concerning the sacrificial service. After the completion of the tabernacle He communicated with Moses from the cloud of glory above the mercy seat, and gave him full directions concerning the *system of offerings and the forms of worship* to be maintained *in the sanctuary. The ceremonial law was thus given to Moses, and by him written in a book*" (PP 364.3).

But, you ask, was not all the "law of Moses" nailed to the cross in Colossians 2? "Blotting out the handwriting of ordinances that was against us, which was contrary to us, and took it out of the way, nailing it to his cross" (Col. 2:14). No, it wasn't!

"The ceremonial system was made up of *symbols pointing to Christ*, to *His sacrifice* and *His priesthood*. This *ritual law*, with *its sacrifices* and *ordinances*, was to be *performed by the Hebrews* until type met antitype in the death of Christ, the Lamb of God that taketh away the sin of the world. Then all the *sacrificial offerings* were to cease. *It is this law* that Christ 'took ... out of the way, nailing it to His cross' " (PP 365.1).

Note: *Nothing else* is mentioned as being part of the ceremonial law!

Ellen G. White comments: "The ceremonial law was given by Christ. Even after it was no longer to be observed, Paul presented it before the Jews in its true position and value,

> " The ceremonial system was made up of symbols pointing to Christ, to His sacrifice and His priesthood. "

showing its place in the plan of redemption and its relation to the work of Christ; and the great apostle pronounces this law glorious, worthy of its divine Originator. *The solemn service of the sanctuary typified* the grand truths that were to be revealed through successive generations. The cloud of incense ascending with the prayers of Israel represents His righteousness that alone can make the sinner's prayer acceptable to God; the bleeding victim on the altar of sacrifice testified of a Redeemer to come; and from the holy of holies the visible token of the divine Presence shone forth" (PP 367.2).

Note: All the ceremonial law took place in the "sanctuary" and had to do with "forms of worship," "offerings," and "symbols pointing to Christ" (see AA 78, 189.3; 190.1, 2; PK 684.3; 685.1, 2; 687.1; 699.1; 705.1; 708.2; PP 367.2; DA 52.2; 608.1, 2).

"The rebellion of Israel against the law and authority of God, caused their destruction. The honor God had given them of being thus conducted by his Son, increased their sin. The charges of the Jews that Christ did not regard the law of Moses, was without the least foundation. Christ was a Jew, and, to the hour of his death upon the cross, observed the law binding upon the Jews. But when type met antitype, at the death of Christ, then the *offering of the blood of beasts became valueless*. Christ made the one great offering in giving his own life, which all their former offerings had foreshadowed, which terminated the value of all the *sacrificial offerings of the Jewish law*" (*Review and Herald*, April 29, 1875, par. 2).

The Moral Law

"*There are two distinct laws brought to view*. One is the law of types and shadows, which reached to the time of Christ, and ceased when type met antitype in his death. The other is the law of Jehovah, and is as abiding and changeless as his eternal throne. After the crucifixion, it was a denial of Christ for the Jews to continue to offer the *burnt offerings* and *sacrifices which were typical of his death*. It was saying to the world that they looked for a Redeemer to come, and had no faith in Him who had given his life for the sins of the world. Hence the ceremonial law ceased to be of force at the death of Christ" (*The Signs of the Times*, July 29, 1886, par. 4).

"Christ passed through all the experiences of His childhood, youth, and manhood *without* the observance of *ceremonial temple* worship" (*The Bible Echo*, Oct. 31, 1898, par. 7).

Note: Jesus never kept the ceremonial law "in His childhood, youth, and manhood"!

Since, *"there are only two laws," everything Christ taught and practiced* is part of the *moral law*.

"Thou camest down also upon mount Sinai, and spakest with them from heaven, and gavest them right judgments, and true laws, good statutes and commandments: and madest known unto them thy holy sabbath, and commandedst them precepts, statutes, and laws, by the hand of Moses thy servant" (Neh. 9:13, 14).

"In consequence of continual transgression, the moral law was repeated in awful grandeur from Sinai. *Christ* gave to Moses religious precepts which were to govern the everyday life. These *statutes* were explicitly given to *guard the ten commandments. They were not shadowy types to pass away with the death of Christ*. They were to be binding upon man in every age as long as time should last. These commands were enforced by the power of the *moral law*, and they clearly and definitely *explained that law*" (*Review and Herald*, May 6, 1875, par. 10).

> " Since, "there are only two laws," everything Christ taught and practiced is part of the moral law. "

"The *statutes and judgments* specifying the duty of man to his fellow-men, were full of important instruction, *defining* and *simplifying* the *principles of the moral law*, for the purpose of increasing religious knowledge, and of preserving God's chosen people distinct and separate from idolatrous nations.

"The necessity of this to preserve the people of God from becoming like the nations who had not the love and fear of God, is the same in this corrupt age, when the transgression of God's law prevails and idolatry exists to a fearful extent. *If ancient Israel needed such security, we need it more, to keep us from being utterly confounded with the transgressors of*

God's law. The hearts of men are so prone to depart from God that there is a necessity for restraint and discipline" (*Review and Herald*, May 6, 1875, par. 5, 6).

Why is this important? Because, *if we believe that the half of the law that explains and reveals the details of the other half of the law was somehow destroyed by Christ on the cross, then we redefine sin, and that cannot be.* Christ died, because the law could not be changed. God's law is immutable.

"The Saviour said nothing to unsettle faith in the religion and institutions that had been given through Moses; for every ray of divine light that Israel's great leader communicated to his people was received from Christ. While many are saying in their hearts that He has come to do away with the law, Jesus in unmistakable language reveals His attitude toward the divine statutes. 'Think not,' He said, 'that I am come to destroy the law, or the prophets.' [Matt. 5:17]" (MB 47.1).

Conclusion

Therefore, Christ is the Author of the writings given to Moses to explain and teach the law. *The moral law contains not only the Ten Precepts but most of the Mosaic law, consisting of the statutes, judgments, testimonies, and God's words*; and obedience to ALL of God's *requirements* are required for salvation.

If we redefine sin according to our reasoning, then, when Jesus comes, will He recognize us? No! The law, *the whole law*, is what we will be judged by. But, you ask, "Aren't we under the new covenant?" Yes, we are. So, let's take a look at that.

CHAPTER 4

THE NEW COVENANT

"As the Bible presents two laws, one changeless and eternal, the other provisional and temporary, so there are two covenants. The *covenant of grace* was first made with man in Eden, when after the Fall there was given a divine promise that the seed of the woman should bruise the serpent's head. To all men this covenant offered pardon and the assisting grace of God for future obedience through faith in Christ. It also promised them eternal life on condition of fidelity to God's law. Thus, the patriarchs received the hope of salvation.

"This same covenant was renewed to Abraham in the promise, 'In thy seed shall all the nations of the earth be blessed.' Genesis 22:18. This promise pointed to Christ. So Abraham understood it [see Gal. 3:8, 16], and he trusted in Christ for the forgiveness of sins. *It was this faith that was accounted unto him for righteousness*. The covenant with Abraham also maintained the authority of God's law. The Lord appeared unto Abraham, and said, 'I am the Almighty God; walk before Me, and be thou perfect.' Genesis 17:1. The testimony of God concerning His faithful servant was, '*Abraham obeyed My voice, and kept My charge, My commandments, My statutes, and My laws.*' Genesis 26:5. And the Lord declared to him, 'I will establish My covenant between Me and thee and thy seed after thee in their generations, for an *everlasting covenant,* to be a God unto thee and to thy seed *after* thee.' Genesis 17:7.

"Though this covenant was made with Adam and renewed to Abraham, it could not be ratified until the death of Christ. It had existed by the promise of God since the first intimation of redemption had been given; it had been accepted by faith; yet when ratified by Christ, it is called a *new* covenant. *The law of God was the basis of this covenant, which was simply an arrangement for bringing men again into harmony with the divine will, placing them where they could obey God's law"* (PP 370.2–4).

"God brought them to Sinai; He manifested His glory; He gave them His law, with the promise of great blessings on condition of obedience: 'If ye will obey My voice indeed, and keep My covenant, then . . . ye shall be unto Me a kingdom of priests, and an holy nation.' Exodus 19:5, 6. The people did not realize the sinfulness of their own hearts, and that without Christ it was impossible for them to keep God's law.

"The 'new covenant' was established upon 'better promises'—the promise of forgiveness of sins and of the grace of God to renew the heart and bring it into harmony with the principles of God's law. 'This shall be the covenant that I will make with the house of Israel; after those days, saith the Lord, *I will put my law* [*torah*] in their inward parts, *and write it in their hearts*. . . . I will *forgive* their iniquity, and will remember their sin no more.' Jeremiah 31:33, 34" (PP 371.4–372.1).

In Hebrews 8:8–12, the writer of Hebrews quotes Jeremiah the prophet: "... Behold, the days come, saith the Lord, when I will make a new covenant with the house of Israel and with the house of Judah: not according to the covenant that I made with their fathers in the day when I took them by the hand to lead them out of the land of Egypt; because they continued not in my covenant, and I regarded them not, saith the Lord. For this is the covenant that I will make with the house of Israel after those days, saith the Lord; I will put *my laws* into their mind, and write them in their hearts: and I will be to them a God, and they shall be to me a people: and they shall not teach every man his neighbour, and every man his brother, saying, Know the Lord: for all shall know me, from the least to the greatest. For I will be merciful to their unrighteousness, and their sins and their iniquities will I remember no more" (Heb. 8:8–12).

And, again, in Hebrews 10:16, 17: "This is the covenant that I will make with them after those days, saith the Lord, I will put *my laws* into their hearts, and in their minds will I write them; and their sins and iniquities will I remember no more" (Heb. 10:16, 17).

Now, here, Paul almost quotes Jeremiah 31:31–34 in its entirety, with a couple of differences in Hebrews 8:8–12 and again in Hebrews 10:16, 17, where he quotes Jeremiah in a more abbreviated form. One of the differences is that Paul says *"laws,"* instead of law, as it is in Jeremiah. Why? In Jeremiah, the word translated as law is *torah*, and *torah* includes *all of the laws, commandments, statutes, testimonies* and *judgments*. If he was only talking about the Ten Commandments, there was no need to quote Jeremiah. So, the law God will write on our hearts is His *torah*. That is how scripture reads. Paul equates *nomos* with *torah*. This changes how we look at the rest of the New Testament, or, at least, how we look at Paul's writings.

Regarding God placing his law in our heart, David, speaking on behalf of Christ, states: "Then said I, Lo, I come: in the volume of the book it is written of me, I delight to do thy will, O my God: yea, thy law [*torah*] is within my heart" (Ps. 40:7, 8). Christ is our example in all things, even in the New Covenant.

In Galatians 2:16, Paul tells us: "Knowing that a man is not justified by the works of the law, but by the faith of Jesus Christ, even we have believed in Jesus Christ, that we might be justified by the faith of Christ, and not by the works of the law: for by the works of the law shall no flesh be justified" (Gal. 2:16). Is this true?

Yes, but so is Galatians 2:17: "But if, while we seek to be justified by Christ, we ourselves also are found sinners, is therefore Christ the minister of sin? God forbid" (Gal. 2:17).

This understanding of the law does not change *how* we are saved. The process of our salvation is the same as it has always been. However, *how* we view the law should guide our understanding of the standard of righteousness and *what* sin is. So, what is the definition of sin? God's Word clearly tells us:

1. "Therefore to him that knoweth to do good, and doeth it not, to him it is sin" (James 4:17).
2. "Whatsoever is not of faith is sin" (Rom. 14:23).
3. "If ye were blind, ye should have no sin: but now ye say, We see; therefore your sin remaineth" (John 9:41).
4. "He will reprove the world of sin, … Of sin, because they believe not on me" (John 16:8, 9).
5. "And it come to pass, when he heareth the words of this curse, that he bless himself in his heart, saying, I shall have peace, though I walk in the imagination ["stubbornness," H8307] of mine heart, to add drunkenness to thirst: the LORD will not spare him, but then the anger of the LORD and his jealousy shall smoke against that man, and all the curses that are written in this book shall lie upon him, and the LORD shall blot out his name from under heaven" (Deut. 29:19, 20).
6. "For rebellion is as the sin of witchcraft, and *stubbornness* is as *iniquity* and idolatry. Because thou hast rejected the word of the LORD, he hath also rejected thee …" (1 Sam. 15:23).

7. "Whosoever committeth sin transgresseth also the law: for sin is the *transgression of the law*" (1 John 3:4).

Note: So, we can see from these verses that:

1. Ignoring what we should do is sin.
2. Whatever we do that isn't of faith is sin.
3. The arrogance and resulting spiritual blindness, which comes from thinking that you know it all [think "Laodicea"], is sin.
4. Not believing on Jesus is sin.
5. Stubbornness is sin. See #3, #6.
6. Rebellion is sin.
7. Transgression of the law is sin.

If *the definition of the law was changed*, 1700 years ago, at the First Council of Nicaea, does that change *God's* definition of sin? No, it does not!

"God's law is the transcript of his character, and those only who obey this law will be accepted by him. Every departure from obedience to the law of God is *rebellion*. It is for the highest interest of man to obey the law of God; for conformity to the principles of this law is essential to the formation of a righteous character. The rules of life that the Lord has given will make men pure and happy and holy. Those only who obey these rules can hear from the lips of Christ the words, 'Come up higher.' [Luke 14:10]" (*Review and Herald*, March 15, 1906, par. 18).

> **"**
> If *the definition of the law was changed*, 1700 years ago, at the First Council of Nicaea, does that change God's definition of sin? No, it does not!
> **"**

So, *submission* to God's *torah*, *or rebellion* to it, is the choice. God's Word states that, just like in Daniel 9 and Psalm 119, we must be in submission to God's *commandments*, His *statutes*, His *judgments*, His *testimonies,* and *His Word*. Most of Christianity no longer believes in dispensationalism. In other words, what was sin is *still* sin. In Daniel 9, Daniel prays a prayer of repentance, "O Lord, to us belongeth confusion of face, to our kings, to our princes, and to our fathers, because we have *sinned* against *thee*. To the Lord our God belong mercies and forgivenesses, though we have *rebelled* against him; neither have we obeyed the voice of the LORD our God, to walk in *his laws* [torah, H8451], which he set before us by his servants the prophets. Yea, all Israel have transgressed *thy law (torah), even by departing*, that they might not obey *thy* voice; therefore the *curse* ["imprecation," H423] is poured upon us, and the oath that is *written in the law of Moses* the servant of God, because we have *sinned* against him. And he hath confirmed his words, which he spake against us, and against our judges that judged us, by bringing upon us a great evil: for under the whole heaven hath not been done as hath been done upon Jerusalem. *As it is written in the law of Moses*, all this evil is come upon us: yet made we not our prayer before the LORD our God, that we might turn from our *iniquities*, and understand *thy truth* [H571]" (Dan. 9:8–13; compare Deut. 29:19–21).

In Daniel's prayer in Daniel 9:10–13, he confesses Israel's transgression of the *Torah* [H8451] and the curse [H423] being poured upon them. As written in the *Torah* [H8451], Jerusalem received the judgments of God *because of their sin*. Ellen White comments: "He [Daniel] pleaded for the honor of God to be preserved. In his petition he identified himself fully with those who had fallen short of the divine purpose, confessing their *sins* as his own" (PK 554.3).

In Scripture, what does it say constitutes the breaking of the covenant?

"But if ye will not hearken unto me, and will not do all these commandments; and if ye shall despise my statutes, or if your soul abhor my judgments, so that ye will not do all my commandments, but that ye break my covenant" (Lev. 26:14, 15).

Moses then goes on for twenty-seven verses, describing the desolation that will occur, if the covenant is broken. Then, he states in verse 43: "… they shall accept of the punishment of their iniquity: because, even because they despised my judgments, and because their soul abhorred my statutes" (Lev. 26:43).

In verse 44, hope is offered for those who broke the covenant: "And yet for all that, when they be in the land of their enemies, I will not cast them away, neither will I abhor them, to destroy them utterly, and to break my covenant with them: for I am the LORD their God" (Lev. 26:44).

CHAPTER 5

THE CURSES

What can we learn from the curse [H423], regarding the law? This curse [H423] is mentioned seventeen times in the Old Testament:

- Four times it is described as a sin to wish on someone.
- Four times it describes the results of an unfaithful wife to her husband.
- Nine times it is used to describe the curse from the book of Deuteronomy, chapters 28 and 29, for *disobedience to God's commandments and statutes.*

The word rendered "curse, curses, or cursing," [H423], defines in the Old Testament, the *verbal* curse or imprecation of God for disobedience to the commandments and statutes of God (see Deut. 28:15–68). In Deuteronomy 29:1, God states that the words in Deuteronomy 28 are a covenant. In verses 14 and 15, God states that *He makes this covenant* not only with Israel but *also with us.* In verses 18 to 21, God uses "curse" to describe what will happen to the rebellious and disobedient among us. We will examine in the following texts the word's meaning in our lives, as we approach the end of time and the judgment.

There are other curses. This curse is an imprecation, a verbal curse by a God who can create with words. The word "curse" [H423] is only used in the Bible to reference the "law of Moses" or the judgment at the end of time. It was considered a sin to wish this on another person (see Job 31:30; Ps. 10:7; Ps. 59:12; Prov. 29:24).

Moses and the Curses

"And the LORD thy God will put all these *curses* [H423] upon thine enemies, and on them that hate thee, which persecuted thee. And thou shalt return and obey the voice of the LORD, and do all *his commandments* which I command thee this day. If thou shalt hearken unto the voice of the LORD thy God, *to keep his commandments* and *his statutes* which are written in this book of the law, and if thou turn unto the LORD thy God with all thine heart, and with all thy soul. For this commandment which I command thee this day, it is not hidden from thee, neither is it far off. See, I have set before thee this day *life* and *good*, and *death* and *evil*; in that I command thee this day to love the LORD thy God, to walk in his ways, and to *keep his commandments* and *his statutes* and *his judgments*, that thou mayest live and multiply: and the LORD thy God shall bless thee in the land whither thou goest to possess it" (Deut. 30:7, 8, 10, 11, 15, 16).

Note: This is where the curse belongs—on our enemies.

Isaiah and the Curses

Isaiah, in his book, refers to the curse when he speaks about the end of time and the judgment: "The earth also is defiled under the inhabitants thereof; because they have transgressed the *laws* [*torah*, H8451], changed the *ordinance* ["statute," H2706], broken the *everlasting* [H5769] covenant. Therefore hath the *curse* ["imprecation," H423] devoured the earth, and they that dwell therein are *desolate* ["guilty," H816]: therefore the inhabitants of the earth are burned, and few men left" (Isa. 24:5, 6).

Regarding the text in Isaiah 24:5, 6:

A. The *Torah* [H8451] is the entire law.
B. The *statutes* [H2706] are the enactments of God, the details of the moral law found in the "laws of Moses." Isaiah states that the earth is defiled because the statutes were changed. *Think;* which statutes were changed?
C. The Sabbath is an everlasting covenant, as indicated in Exodus 31:16, 17, where the word "everlasting" [H5769] is rendered "perpetual."
Isaiah states that the earth is defiled because the Sabbath is broken:
"Wherefore the children of Israel shall keep the sabbath, to observe the sabbath throughout their generations, for a *perpetual*

["everlasting," H5769] covenant. It is a sign between me and the children of Israel *for ever* ["everlasting," H5769]: for in six days the LORD made heaven and earth, and on the seventh day he rested, and was refreshed" (Exod. 31:16, 17).
D. The imprecation is the curse on the other side of the scroll in Zechariah 5:3, and the curse threatened in Deuteronomy 29.

Zechariah and the Curses

There are three rolls in Scripture that are written on both sides. They are found in Zechariah 5, Ezekiel 2, and Revelation 5. Each is concerned with the judgment and the end of time.

In this brief review, we will be dealing primarily with the roll in Zechariah 5.

"Then said he unto me, This is the *curse* ["imprecation," H423] that goeth forth over the face of the whole earth: for every one that stealeth shall be cut off as on this side according to it; and every one that *sweareth* shall be cut off as on that side according to it" (Zech. 5:3). This scroll, written on both sides, is found in Zechariah 5:1-4.

The *statute* for swearing falsely is found in Leviticus 6:3, 5; 19:12, 37.

"Or have found that which was lost, and lieth concerning it, and *sweareth falsely*; in any of all these that a man doeth, sinning therein: or all that about which he hath *sworn falsely*; he shall even restore it in the principal, and shall add the fifth part more thereto, and give it unto him to whom it appertaineth, in the day of his trespass offering" (Lev. 6:3, 5).

"And ye shall not swear by my name falsely, neither shalt thou profane the name of thy God: I am the LORD. Thou shalt not defraud thy neighbour, neither rob him: the wages of him that is hired shall not abide with thee all night until the morning. ... Therefore shall ye observe all my statutes, and all my judgments, and do them: I am the LORD." (Lev. 19:12, 13, 37).

One side of the roll is devoted to the law of Moses as typified by the following statutes:

"And he said unto me, It is done. I am Alpha and Omega, the beginning and the end. I will give unto him that is athirst of the fountain of the water of life freely. He that overcometh shall inherit all things; and I will be his God, and he shall be my son. But the *fearful* [Deut. 3:22], and *unbelieving* [Num. 14:11], and the abominable, and murderers, and *whoremongers* [Lev. 21:7, 9], and *sorcerers* [Deut. 18:10, Exod. 22:18], and idolaters, and all *liars* [Lev. 6:1–5; 19:12], shall have their part in the lake which burneth with fire and brimstone: which is the second death" (Rev. 21:6–8).

The other side is devoted to the ten precepts, as typified by the eighth commandment, "Thou shalt not steal" (Exod. 20:15). The entire moral law is thus shown to be the standard of the judgment and what awaits those who have offended God's holy law.

Ellen White comments on Zechariah 5:4, its connection to the three angels' message, and the *binding claims of the law of God*. Here is typified, with these two examples, the judgment at the end of time and that which awaits those who have offended either the law of Moses or the ten precepts.

" 'I turned, and lifted up mine eyes, and looked, and behold a flying roll.... This is the curse that goeth forth over the face of the whole earth: for everyone that *stealeth* shall be cut off as on this side according to it; and everyone that *sweareth* shall be cut off as on that side according to it. I will bring it forth, saith the Lord of hosts, and it shall enter into the house of the *thief*, and into the house of him that *sweareth falsely* by My name: and it shall remain in the midst of his house, and shall consume it with the timber thereof and the stones thereof.' Zechariah 5:1–4.

"Against every evildoer *God's law* utters condemnation. He may disregard that voice, he may seek to drown its warning, but in vain. It follows him. It makes itself heard. It destroys his peace. If unheeded, it pursues him to the grave. It bears witness against him at the judgment. A quenchless fire, it consumes at last soul and body" (Ed 144.4, 5).

"The Spirit who asked Zechariah, 'What seest thou?' to which he answered, 'I see a flying roll,' also caused an angel to fly in the midst of heaven, 'having the everlasting gospel to preach unto them that dwell on the earth, and to every nation, and kindred and tongue, and people, saying with a loud voice, Fear God, and give glory to Him [let no glory be given to erring, sinful men]; for the hour of His judgment is come.' *Many indeed will not understand, but will stumble at the words contained in the roll*" (*Special Testimonies*, Series B, No.7, p. 60, par. 2).

Note: Brother and sister, do not stumble over this message.

"When God sends a message to any person, ... if men pursue a course to make of no effect the message sent, a course that destroys the influence of the message that God designed should make a change in the principles of the one corrected, and turn his heart to repentance, it would be better for these men if they had never been born" (*Special Testimonies*, Series B, No.7, p. 59, par. 2).

Josiah and the Curses

The Curses in Chronicles

In 2 Chronicles 34–35:1, we see the story of Josiah who has the book of the law brought to him and hears the requirements of God for salvation and the results of not keeping "the word of the Lord, to do after all that is written in this book." He found that they were subject to "even all the *curses* that are written in the book." The story tells us of his horror and inquiring of the Lord regarding Hulda the prophetess, of his ultimate surrender to God, and of the covenant that he makes with God "to keep His *commandments*, and His *testimonies*, and His *statutes*, with all his heart and with all his soul to perform the words of the covenant which are written in this book."

"For there is no respect of persons with God. For as many as have sinned without law shall also perish without law: and as many as have sinned in the law shall be judged by the law; (*For not the hearers of the law are just before God, but the doers of the law shall be justified*)" (Rom. 2:11–13).

Whether in Josiah's day, Paul's day, or ours, God and His laws have not changed or been annulled. God's law is His *torah*.

Ellen White writes regarding a reform movement that took place during Josiah's reign: "This reform movement, by which threatened judgments were averted for a season, was brought about in a wholly unexpected manner through the discovery and study of a portion of Holy Scripture that for many years *had been strangely misplaced and lost.*

> "Whether in Josiah's day, Paul's day, or ours, God and His laws have not changed or been annulled."

"Nearly a century before, during the first Passover celebrated by Hezekiah, provision had been made for the daily public reading of the book of the law to the people by teaching priests. *It was the observance of the statutes recorded by Moses, especially those given in the book of the covenant, which forms a part of Deuteronomy, that had made the reign of Hezekiah so prosperous.* But Manasseh had dared set aside *these statutes*; and during his reign the temple copy of the book of the law, through careless neglect, had become lost. Thus for many years the people generally were deprived of its instruction" (PK 392.1–392.2).

Nehemiah and the Curses

"They clave to their brethren, their nobles, and entered into a *curse,* and into an oath, to *walk in God's law,* which was given by Moses the servant of God, and to *observe* and do all the *commandments* of the LORD our Lord, and his *judgments* and his *statutes*" (Neh. 10:29).

In Nehemiah 9:13, 14, we read: "Thou camest down also upon mount Sinai, and spakest with them from heaven, and gavest them *right judgments,* and *true laws, good statutes* and *commandments:* and madest known unto them thy holy sabbath, and commandedst them precepts, statutes, and laws, by the hand of Moses thy servant."

In *Patriarchs and Prophets,* page 365, Ellen White quotes this same text and emphasizes the whole phrase, *"right judgments, and true laws, good statutes and commandments."*

"Let thine ear now be attentive, and thine eyes open, that thou mayest hear the prayer of thy servant, which I pray before thee now, day and night, for the children of Israel thy servants, and confess the sins of the children of Israel, which we have sinned against thee: both I and my father's house have sinned. We have dealt very corruptly against thee, and have not kept the commandments, nor the statutes, nor the judgments, which thou commandedst thy servant Moses" (Neh. 1:6, 7).

Regarding the work of restoration, we read:

"The work of restoration and reform carried on by the returned exiles, under the leadership of Zerubbabel, Ezra, and Nehemiah, presents a picture of a work of spiritual restoration that is to be wrought in the closing days of this earth's history. The remnant of Israel were a feeble people, exposed to the ravages of their enemies; but through them God purposed to preserve in the earth a knowledge of Himself and of His law.

"The *spiritual restoration of which the work carried forward in Nehemiah's day* was a symbol, is outlined in the words of Isaiah: 'They shall build the old wastes, they shall raise up the former desolations, and they shall repair the waste cities.' 'They that shall be of thee shall build the old waste places: thou shalt raise up the foundations of many generations; and thou shalt be called, The repairer of the breach, the restorer of paths to dwell in.' Isaiah 61:4; 58:12.

"The prophet here describes a people who, in a time of general departure from truth and righteousness, are seeking to restore the *principles that are the foundation of the kingdom of God. They are repairers of a breach that has been made in God's law—the wall that He has placed around His chosen ones for their protection, and obedience to whose precepts of justice, truth, and purity is to be their perpetual safeguard"* (PK 677.1–3; see PP 311.2).

Jesus Speaks of the Curses

The curse that was poured out is also mentioned by Christ in the book of Matthew. Speaking of the judgment and the results of ignoring the mandates of the Mosaic Law, Jesus states: "Depart from me, ye *cursed* ["imprecation," G2672], into everlasting fire, prepared for the devil and his angels" (Matt. 25:41). Jesus makes this command after discussing the obligation of the Mosaic Law: "For I was an hungred, and ye gave me meat: I was thirsty, and ye gave me drink: I was a stranger, and ye took me in: naked, and ye clothed me: I was sick, and ye visited me: I was in prison, and ye came unto me. Then shall the righteous answer him, saying, Lord, when saw we thee an hungred, and fed thee? or thirsty, and gave thee drink?" (Matt. 25:35–37; see also Lev. 23:22; 25:6, 35; Deut. 10:18; 14:29; 16:14; 26:11–13).

In Mark 11:21, Peter uses this same word "cursed" in describing Jesus' cursing of the fig tree, which represents God's *professed* people who are lost.

"Besides the coming of the Lord to His temple, Malachi also foretells *His second advent*, His coming for the *execution of the judgment*, in these words: 'And I will come near to you to judgment; and I will be a swift witness against the *sorcerers*, and against the adulterers, and against *false swearers*, and against those that *oppress the hireling in his wages, the widow*, and *the fatherless*, and that *turn aside the stranger from his right*, and fear not Me, saith the Lord of hosts.' Malachi 3:5" (GC 425.3).

References to the Mosaic Law, mentioned in the above statements, are Exodus 22:18; Leviticus 6:3; 19:12, 13; Deuteronomy 10:18; 14:29; 16:11; 18:10.

Note: The statutes are involved in the judgment at the end of time.

CHAPTER 6

WHO KEPT THE STATUTES?

Abraham

"'Abraham believed God, and it was imputed unto him for righteousness: and he was called the friend of God.' James 2:23. And Paul says, 'They which are of faith, the same are the children of Abraham.' Galatians 3:7. But Abraham's faith was made manifest by his works. 'Was not Abraham our father justified by works, when he had offered Isaac his son upon the altar? Seest thou how faith wrought with his works, and by works was faith made perfect.?' James 2:21, 22. There are many who fail to understand the relation of faith and works. They say, 'Only believe in Christ, and you are safe. You have nothing to do with keeping the law.' But genuine faith will be manifest in obedience. Said Christ to the unbelieving Jews, 'If ye were Abraham's children, ye would do the works of Abraham.' John 8:39. And concerning the father of the faithful the Lord declares, 'Abraham obeyed *My voice*, and *kept My charge*, *My commandments*, *My statutes*, and *My laws*.' Genesis 26:5. Says the apostle James, 'Faith, if it hath not works, is dead, being alone.' James 2:17. And John, who dwells so fully upon love, tells us, 'This is the love of God, that we keep His commandments.' John 5:3" (PP 153.4).

How do we know that Abraham kept the same statutes that Moses and the children of Israel did? Moses wrote all five books of the Torah, and he used the same Hebrew words to describe both the statutes that Abraham kept and the statutes that Moses and the Israelites kept.

Joseph

"Blow up the trumpet in the new moon, in the time appointed, on our solemn feast day. For this was a statute [H2708] for Israel, and a law of the God of Jacob. This he ordained in Joseph for a testimony, when he went out through the land of Egypt" (Ps. 81:3–5). The Feast of Trumpets is the only feast that falls on the new moon.

Note: Critics have said that this text doesn't apply to Joseph personally but to Israel as a whole. However, the timing of David's statement places the keeping of the statute of trumpets prior to the giving of the ceremonial law.

Moses

"But it shall come to pass, if thou wilt not hearken unto the voice of the LORD thy God, to observe to do all his *commandments* and his *statutes* which I command thee this day; that all these curses shall come upon thee, and overtake thee: Moreover all these curses shall come upon thee, and shall pursue thee, and overtake thee, till thou be destroyed; because thou hearkenedst not unto the voice of the LORD thy God, to keep his commandments and his statutes which he commanded thee" (Deut. 28:15, 45).

Note: To receive the blessings, keep the commandments (Deut. 28:1–14). To *not* receive the curses, keep the commandments *and* the statutes. (Deut. 28:15–68).

> "But it shall come to pass, if thou wilt not hearken unto the voice of the LORD thy God, to observe to do all his commandments and his statutes which I command thee this day; that all these curses shall come upon thee, and overtake thee."

"If thou shalt hearken unto the voice of the LORD thy God, to keep his *commandments* and his *statutes* which are written in this *book of the law*, and if thou turn unto the LORD thy God with all thine heart, and with all thy soul. For this commandment which I command thee this day, it is not hidden from thee, *neither is it far off* [meaning, *"it's not too difficult,"* as translated in the New American Standard Bible, 1995]" (Deut. 30:11).

"Sanctify yourselves therefore, and be ye holy: for I am the LORD your God. And ye shall keep my *statutes*, and do them: I am the LORD which *sanctify* you" (Lev. 20:7, 8).

Note: Ezekiel and Moses declare that the keeping of the *statutes* is required for sanctification (see the section on Ezek. 20:11, 12, 19–24 in this chapter).

"Speak thou also unto the children of Israel, saying, Verily my sabbaths ye shall keep: for it is a sign between me and you throughout your generations; that ye may know that I am the LORD that doth *sanctify* you" (Exod. 31:13).

"To this people were committed the oracles of God. They were hedged about by the precepts of His law, the everlasting principles of truth, justice, and purity. Obedience to these principles was to be their protection, for it would save them from destroying themselves by sinful practices.

"Through Moses the purpose of God was set before them and the terms of their prosperity made plain. 'Thou art an holy people unto the Lord thy God,' he said; 'the Lord thy God hath chosen thee to be a special people unto Himself, above all people that are upon the face of the earth' " (PK 18.1–19.3).

" 'Thou hast avouched the Lord this day to be thy God, and to walk in *His ways*, and to *keep His statutes*, and *His commandments, and His judgments*, and to *hearken unto His voice*: and the Lord hath avouched thee this day to be His peculiar people, as He hath promised thee, and that thou shouldest keep *all His commandments*; and to make thee high above all nations which He hath made, in praise, and in name, and in honor; and that thou mayest be an holy people unto the Lord thy God, as He hath spoken.' Deuteronomy 7:6; 26:17–19" (PK 18.4).

Speaking of Moses' vision at his death, Ellen G. White states:

"He had been shown the work of Satan in leading the Jews to reject Christ, while they professed to honor His Father's law. He now saw the Christian world under a similar deception in professing to accept Christ while they rejected God's law. He had heard from the priests and elders the frenzied cry, 'Away with Him!' 'Crucify Him, crucify Him!' and now he heard from professedly Christian teachers the cry, 'Away with the law!' He saw the Sabbath trodden under foot, and a spurious institution established in its place. Again Moses was filled with astonishment and horror. *How could those who believed in Christ reject the law spoken by His own voice upon the sacred mount*? How could any that feared God set aside the law which is the foundation of His government in heaven and earth? With joy Moses saw the law of God still honored and exalted by a faithful few. He saw the last great struggle of earthly powers to destroy those who keep God's law" (PP 476.2; see Neh. 9:13, 14).

" 'What nation is there so great, who hath God so nigh unto them, as the Lord our God is in all things that we call upon Him for? And what nation is there so great, that hath statutes and judgments so righteous as all this law, which I set before you this day?' Deuteronomy 4:7, 8. *Today the challenge to Israel might be repeated*" (PP 465.1).

> " *How could those who believed in Christ reject the law spoken by His own voice upon the sacred mount?* "

Note: *What law is Moses and Ellen White talking about*? (see Deut. 4:5, 6).

" 'This day the Lord thy God hath commanded thee to do these *statutes* and *judgments*: thou shalt therefore keep and do them with all thine heart, and with all thy soul. Thou hast avouched the Lord this day to be thy God, and to walk in His ways, and to keep His *statutes*, and His *commandments*, and His *judgments*, and to hearken unto His voice.' [Deuteronomy 26:16, 17.] This is not the voice of man. *It is the voice of Christ* from the infolding pillar of cloud. *Read carefully all of Deuteronomy 26, also chapters 27 and 28; for here are stated plainly the blessings of obedience.*

"These directions, which the Lord has given to His people, express the principles of the law of the kingdom of God; and they are made specific, so that the minds of the people may not be left in ignorance and uncertainty. These Scriptures present the *never-ceasing* obligation of all whom God has blessed with life and health and advantages in temporal and spiritual things. The message has not grown weak because of age. God's claims are just as binding now, just as fresh in their importance, as God's gifts are fresh and continual" (Ms. 67, 1907, par. 3, 4).

Joshua

"Only be thou strong and very courageous, that thou mayest observe to do according to *all the law*, which Moses my servant commanded thee: turn not from it to the right hand or to the left, that thou mayest prosper withersoever thou goest. This *book of the law* shall not depart out of thy mouth; but thou shalt meditate therein day and night, that thou mayest observe to do according to *all that is written* therein: for then thou shalt make thy way prosperous, and then thou shalt have good success" (Joshua 1:7, 8).

"Be ye therefore very courageous to keep and to do all that is written in *the book of the law* of Moses, that ye turn not aside therefrom to the right hand or to the left" (Joshua 23:6).

"And if it seem evil unto you to serve the LORD, choose you this day whom ye will serve; whether the gods which your fathers served that were on the other side of the flood, or the gods of the Amorites, in whose land ye dwell: but as for me and my house, we will serve the LORD" (Joshua 24:15).

" 'The Lord hath taken you, and brought you forth out of the iron furnace,' declared Moses, 'to be unto Him a people of inheritance.' The land which they were soon to enter, and which was to be theirs on condition of obedience to *the law of God, was thus described to them*" (PP 465.2).

David

"I have inclined mine heart to perform thy *statutes* alway, even unto the end ["heel, last of anything," H6118]" (Ps. 119:112).

"I have seen an end of all perfection: but thy *commandment* is exceeding broad" (Ps. 119:96).

"Salvation is far from the wicked: for they seek not thy *statutes*" (Ps. 119:155).

"For all his *judgments* were before me: and as for his *statutes*, I did not depart from them. I was also upright before him, and have kept myself from mine iniquity" (2 Sam. 22:23, 24).

"Teach me, O LORD, the way of thy *statutes*; and I shall keep it unto the end [H6118]" (Ps. 119:33).

Isaiah

"The earth mourneth and fadeth away, the world languisheth and fadeth away, the haughty people of the earth do languish. The earth also is defiled under the inhabitants thereof; because they have *transgressed the laws* [*torah*, H8451], changed the *ordinance* [statute, H2706], broken the *everlasting covenant*. Therefore hath the *curse* [imprecation, H423] devoured the earth, and they that dwell therein are *desolate* ["guilty," H816]: therefore the inhabitants of the earth are *burned*, and few men left" (Isa. 24:4–6).

Note: This denotes the judgement at the end of time.

"To the law [*torah*] and to the testimony: if they speak not according to this word, it is because there is no light in them" (Isa. 8:20).

Josiah

"And the king (*Josiah*) stood in his place, and made a covenant before the LORD, to walk after the LORD, and to keep his *commandments*, and his *testimonies*, and his *statutes*, with all his heart, and with all his soul, to perform the *words of the covenant* which are written in this book" (2 Chron. 34:31).

"During the reign of Josiah the word of the Lord came to Zephaniah, specifying plainly the results of continued apostasy, and calling the attention of the true church to the glorious prospect beyond. His prophecies of impending judgment upon Judah *apply with equal force to the judgments that are to fall upon an impenitent world at the time of the second advent of Christ*" (PK 389; see "Zephaniah," below).

Jeremiah

"They are not humbled even unto this day, neither have they feared, nor walked in *my law*, nor in *my statutes* [H2706], that I set before you and before your fathers. ... Because ye have burned incense, and because ye have sinned against the LORD, and have not obeyed the voice of the LORD, nor walked in *his law*, nor in *his statutes* [H2706], nor in *his testimonies*; therefore this evil is happened unto you, as at this day" (Jer. 44:10, 23).

Daniel

"O Lord, to us belongeth confusion of face, to our kings, to our princes, and to our fathers, because we have sinned against thee. To the Lord our God belong mercies and forgivenesses, though we have rebelled against him; neither have we obeyed the voice of the LORD our God, to walk in his *laws*, which he set before us by his servants the prophets. Yea, all Israel have transgressed thy *law*, even by departing, that they might not obey thy voice; therefore the curse is poured upon us, and the oath that is written in the law of Moses the servant of God, because we have sinned against him. And he hath confirmed his words, which he spake against us, and against our judges that judged us, by bringing upon us a great evil: for under the whole heaven hath not been done as hath been done upon Jerusalem. As it is written in the *law of Moses*, all this evil is come upon us: yet made we not our prayer before the LORD our God, that we might turn from our iniquities, and understand thy *truth* [H571]" (Dan. 9:8–13).

Ezekiel

We, many times, focus on the Sabbath as a sign, but a careful reading of Ezekiel 20 will show God's *statutes* and *judgments* are also required.

"And I gave them my *statutes*, and shewed them my *judgments*, which if a man do, he shall even live in them. Moreover also I gave them my *sabbaths*, to be a sign between me and them, that they might know that I am the LORD that *sanctify* them" (Ezek. 20:11, 12).

"I am the LORD your God; walk in *my statutes*, and keep *my judgments*, and *do them*; and hallow my *sabbaths*; and they shall be a sign between me and you, that ye may know that I am the LORD your God. Notwithstanding the children rebelled against me: they walked not in my *statutes*, neither kept my *judgments* to do them, which if a man do, he shall even live in them; they *polluted my sabbaths*: then I said, I would pour out my fury upon them, to accomplish my anger against them in the wilderness. Nevertheless I withdrew mine hand, and wrought for my name's sake, that it should not be polluted in the sight of the heathen, in whose sight I brought them forth. I lifted up mine hand unto them also in the wilderness, that I would scatter them among the heathen, and disperse them through the countries; because they had *not executed my judgments*, but had *despised my statutes*, and had *polluted my sabbaths*, and their eyes were after their fathers' idols" (Ezek. 20:19–24).

Note: Both Moses and Ezekiel state the keeping of the Sabbath and statutes are necessary for *sanctification* (see Lev. 20:8 and the section on "Moses and the Curses" in chapter V).

Ezra

"For Ezra had prepared his heart to seek the law of the LORD, and to do it, and to teach in Israel *statutes* and *judgments*. Now this is the copy of the letter that the king Artaxerxes gave unto Ezra the priest, the scribe, even a scribe of the words of the *commandments* of the LORD, and of *his statutes* to Israel. Artaxerxes, king of kings, unto Ezra the priest, *a scribe of the law of the God of heaven*, perfect peace, and at such a time" (Ezra 7:10–12).

"Ezra developed into a man of extraordinary learning and became 'a ready scribe in the *law of Moses*.' [Ezra 7:6.] These qualifications made him an eminent man in the Medo-Persian kingdom. Ezra became a mouthpiece for God, *educating those about him in the principles that govern heaven*" (PK 609.1–2).

Note: The commandments, statutes, and judgments are the principles that govern heaven.

Nehemiah

"We have dealt very corruptly against thee, and have not kept *the commandments*, nor *the statutes*, nor *the judgments*, which thou commandedst thy servant Moses. Remember, I beseech thee, the word that thou commandedst thy servant Moses, saying, If ye transgress, I will scatter you abroad among the nations: but if ye turn unto me, and keep my *commandments*, and do them; though there were of you cast out unto the uttermost part of the heaven, yet will I gather them from thence, and will bring them unto the place that I have chosen to set my name there" (Neh. 1:7–9).

"They clave to their brethren, their nobles, and entered into a *curse* [H423], and into an oath, to walk in God's law, which was given by Moses the servant of God, and to observe and do all the *commandments* of the LORD our Lord, and his *judgments* and his *statutes*" (Neh. 10:29).

Hosea

"My people are destroyed for lack of knowledge: because thou hast rejected knowledge, I will also reject thee, that thou shalt be no priest to me: seeing thou hast forgotten the law [*torah*] of thy God, I will also forget thy children" (Hosea 4:6).

"Set the trumpet to thy mouth. He shall come as an eagle against the house of the LORD, because they have transgressed my covenant, and trespassed against my law [*torah*]" (Hosea 8:1).

"I have written to him the great things of *my law* [*torah*], *but they were counted as a strange thing*" (Hosea 8:12).

Is this a prophetic message regarding the end-time church?

Amos

"Thus saith the LORD; for three transgressions of Judah, and for four, I will not turn away the punishment thereof; because they have despised the law [*torah*] of the LORD, and have not kept his *commandments* ["statutes," H2706], and their *lies* caused them to err, after the which their fathers have walked" (Amos 2:4). The word *law* is *torah* [H8451] and *commandments* is "statutes" [H2706].

Zechariah

"Thus speaketh the LORD of hosts, saying, Execute true [H571] judgment, and shew mercy and compassions every man to his brother: and oppress not the widow, nor the fatherless, the stranger, nor the poor; and let none of you imagine evil against his brother in your heart. But they refused to hearken, and pulled away the shoulder, and stopped their ears, that they should not hear. Yea, they made their hearts as an adamant stone, lest they should hear the law [*torah*], and the words which the LORD of hosts hath sent in his spirit by the former prophets: therefore came a great wrath from the LORD of hosts" (Zech. 7:9–12).

"But my words and *my statutes*, which I commanded my servants the prophets, did they not take hold of your fathers? and they returned and said, Like as the LORD of hosts thought to do unto us, according to our ways, and according to our doings, so hath he dealt with us" (Zech. 1:6).

Zephaniah

Zephaniah prophesied during the reign of Josiah.
(See note on Josiah above.)

"I will gather them that are sorrowful for the solemn *assembly* [*moed*, "appointed time, a statute," H4150], who are of thee, to whom the reproach of it was a burden. Behold, at that time I will undo all that afflict thee: and I will save her that halteth, and gather her that was driven out; and I will get them praise and fame in every land where they have been put to shame" (Zeph. 3:18, 19).

Do we know a group of people who have been afflicted and driven out because of the disgrace of the appointed times [H4150]?

Both the Sabbath and the feasts are *moeds* ["appointed times"] (see Leviticus 23).

Malachi

"The closing words of Malachi are a prophecy regarding the work that should be done preparatory to the *first* and the *second* advent of Christ. This prophecy is introduced with the admonition, '*Remember ye the law of Moses* my servant, which I commanded unto him in Horeb for all Israel, with the statutes and judgments. Behold, I will send you Elijah the prophet before the coming of the great and dreadful day of the Lord; and he shall turn the heart of the fathers to the children, and the heart of the children to their fathers, lest I come and smite the earth with a curse.' [Malachi 4:4–6]" (*The Southern Watchman*, March 21, 1905, par. 1, 2).

Note: Malachi states: "Even from the days of your fathers ye are gone away from mine ordinances, and have not kept them. Return unto me, and I will return unto you, saith the LORD of hosts. But ye said, Wherein shall we return? Will a man rob God? Yet ye have robbed me. But ye say, Wherein have we robbed thee? In tithes and offerings" (Mal. 3:7, 8). *The word "ordinance" is actually "statute"* [H2706]. This means that the same word used in Malachi 4:4 is also used in Malachi 3:7. *If tithe-paying is required for salvation, so are the rest of the statutes!*

> " Remember ye the law of Moses my servant, which I commanded unto him in Horeb for all Israel, with the statutes and judgments. "

In Malachi 2:9, it states that to be partial in the law makes you contemptible in God's eyes: "Therefore have I also made you contemptible and base before all the people, according as *ye have not kept my ways*, but have been *partial* in the law [*torah*]" (Mal. 2:9).

Jesus

David prophesied, *concerning Christ*: "Then said I, Lo, I come: in the volume of the book it is written of me, I delight to do thy will, O my God: yea, thy law [*torah*] is within my heart" (Ps. 40:7, 8).

Matthew 19, Mark 10, and Luke 18 all record the young man coming to Christ asking: "What good thing shall I do, that I may have eternal life?" (Matt. 19:16).

Jesus' answer is recorded slightly differently by each writer.

- Matthew 19:19 lists four commandments and one *statute*: "Thou shalt love thy neighbour as thyself," which is found in Leviticus 19:18.
- Mark 10:19 lists four commandments and a *different statute*: "Defraud not," which is found in Leviticus 19:13.
- Luke lists only commandments.
- But all three gospels list Jesus' instructions concerning the poor, which have their roots in Leviticus 19:10; 23:22; 25:25; and Deuteronomy 15:1–15.

In the Beatitudes, Jesus stated:

"Whosoever therefore shall break one of these *least commandments*, and shall teach men so, he shall be called the least in the kingdom of heaven: but whosoever shall do and teach them, the same shall be called great in the kingdom of heaven" (Matt. 5:19).

If Jesus is not referring to the *statutes*, *judgments*, and *testimonies*, which explain the ten precepts, to what is He referring?

When Jesus was confronted by Satan, Jesus' answers, which were foundational, came from the statutes:

"But he answered and said, *It is written*, Man shall not live by bread alone, but by every word that proceedeth out of the mouth of God. Jesus said unto him, *It is written* again, Thou shalt not tempt the Lord thy God. Then saith Jesus unto him, Get thee hence, Satan: for *it is written*, Thou shalt worship the Lord thy God, and him only shalt thou serve" (Matt. 4:4, 7, 10).

All of Christ's answers came from Deuteronomy 6–8, in which "statutes" are mentioned seven times; "commandments," eight times; "all ... commandments," two times; "judgments," five times; and "testimonies," twice; and "words," once.

In Matthew 25, Jesus tells us of the ten virgins and the talents, and then ends His discourse expounding upon the following statutes in verses 35 to 41:

- Leviticus 25:35
- Deuteronomy 10:17–19
- Leviticus 23:22
- Deuteronomy 26:11–13
- Psalm 36:8

Jesus finishes by explaining the results of ignoring His statutes, repeating the curse that the Mosaic law threatened, which awaits those who ignore His statutes at the end of time; confirming Deuteronomy 28:15, 45, 58, 59; 29:19–21.

Jesus Christ, when speaking of the commandments in Matthew 5:17–19, referred to "the least commandments." At the time He said this; the entire law, including the ceremonial law, was in effect. He stated in verse 18: "Till heaven and earth pass, one jot or one tittle shall in no wise pass from the law till all be fulfilled." Have heaven and earth passed? No! So, what did pass? *The ceremonial law, consisting of sacrifices and offerings, the earthly temple and its services, and the earthly priesthood, was fulfilled,* and all of these prefigured Christ. The goats and lambs that were offered represented Jesus; the priesthood represented Christ as our high priest; the temple service itself was about Christ's mission to save us and pay the ransom for our sins. No law or statute relating to morality, human relationships, or time with God and each other was removed.

The temple service revealed Christ's sacrifice and His continual work in heaven to bring us into oneness with Him. And temple service *continues* in heaven, as shown in the book of Hebrews. The temple service here on earth culminated in the crucifixion and resurrection of our Lord, and its existence in the writings of the Old and New Testaments was the express purpose of showing us the plan of salvation.

The fulfillment of these types of Christ had no power to *change God's law* so dramatically, as Jesus says in Matthew 5:17–19.

Jesus and His Father have a vested interest in how men and women should live in relation to each other within the family structure and in relation to God Himself. How we dress, eat, conduct business, relate to unbelievers, serve God, worship Him, learn to be like Him, and spend time with Him are explained in the entirety of Scripture. Be careful of pastors and teachers who tell you that any of God's laws are not important. Hell awaits those who defy God's laws and statutes, or who trivialize His testimonies, words, or commands.

Paul

"For ye know what commandments we gave you by the Lord Jesus. For this is the will of God, *even your sanctification*, that ye should abstain from *fornication* [Deut. 22:13–21; Lev. 20:8]: that every one of you should know how to possess his vessel in sanctification and honour; not in the lust of concupiscence, even as the Gentiles which know not God: that no man go beyond and *defraud his brother* [Lev. 19:13] in any matter: because that the Lord is the avenger of all such, as we also have forewarned you and testified. For God hath not called us unto uncleanness, but unto holiness. He therefore that despiseth, despiseth not man, but God, who hath also given unto us his holy Spirit" (1 Thess. 4:2–8).

"It is reported commonly that there is fornication among you, and such fornication as is not so much as named among the Gentiles, that one should have his father's wife" (1 Cor. 5:1).

Paul had received his training from the *Torah*: "Cursed be he that lieth with his father's wife" (Deut. 27:20).

"Nay, ye do wrong, and *defraud* [Lev. 19:13], and that your brethren. Know ye not that *the unrighteous shall not inherit the kingdom of God*? Be not deceived: neither *fornicators* [Deut. 22:21], nor *idolaters* [Exod. 20:4], nor adulterers, nor *effeminate* [Lev. 20:13], nor *abusers* of themselves with mankind, nor thieves, nor covetous, nor *drunkards* [Lev. 10:9], nor revilers, nor *extortioners* [Lev. 6:2], shall inherit the kingdom of God. And such were some of you: but ye are washed, but *ye are sanctified* [Lev. 20:8], but ye are justified in the name of the Lord Jesus, and by the Spirit of our God" (1 Cor. 6:8–11).

"For all the law is fulfilled in one word, even in this; thou shalt love thy neighbour as thyself. But if ye bite and devour one another, take heed that ye be not consumed one of another. This I say then, Walk in the Spirit, and ye shall not fulfil the lust of the flesh. For the flesh lusteth against the Spirit, and the Spirit against the flesh: and these are contrary the one to the other: so that ye cannot do the things that ye would. But if ye be led of the Spirit, ye are not under the law. Now the works of the flesh are manifest, which are these; adultery, *fornication* [Deut. 22:21], uncleanness, lasciviousness, idolatry, *witchcraft* [Deut. 18:10], *hatred* [Lev. 19:17], variance, emulations, wrath, strife, seditions, heresies, envyings, murders, *drunkenness* [Lev. 10:9], revellings, and such like: of the which I tell you before, as I have also told you in time past, that *they which do such things shall not inherit the kingdom of God*" (Gal. 5:14–21).

Paul taught the Torah!

"For this cause God gave them up unto vile affections: for even their women did change the natural use into that which is against nature: and likewise also the men, leaving the natural use of the woman, burned in their lust one toward another; men with men working that which is unseemly, and receiving in themselves that recompence of their error which was meet" (Rom. 1:26, 27).

"If a man also lie with mankind, as he lieth with a woman, both of them have committed an abomination: they shall surely be put to death; their blood shall be upon them" (Lev. 20:13).

"Now I praise you, brethren, that ye remember me in all things, and keep the *ordinances* ["Jewish traditionary laws," G3862], as I delivered them to you" (1 Cor. 11:2).

"Now we command you, brethren, in the name of our Lord Jesus Christ, that ye withdraw yourselves from every brother that walketh disorderly, and not after the *tradition* [G3862, same word as ordinances, above, in 1 Corinthians 11:2] which he received of us" (2 Thess. 3:6).

"Therefore, brethren, stand fast, and hold the *traditions* [G3862] which ye have been taught, whether by word, or our epistle" (2 Thess. 2:15).

"And it came to pass, that after three days Paul called the chief of the Jews together: and when they were come together, he said unto them, Men and brethren, though I *have committed nothing against the people, or customs of our fathers*, yet was I delivered prisoner from Jerusalem into the hands of the Romans" (Acts 28:17).

"And we sailed away from Philippi *after the days of unleavened bread*, and came unto them to Troas in five days; where we abode seven days" (Acts 20:6).

"*At Philippi Paul tarried to keep the Passover*. Only Luke remained with him, the other members of the company passing on to Troas to await him there. The Philippians were the most loving and truehearted of the apostle's converts, and during the eight days of the feast he enjoyed peaceful and happy communion with them" (AA 390.4).

Note: This took place involving Gentile believers [a synagogue has never been found in Philippi] approximately 26 years after the crucifixion of Christ in or about spring A.D. 57 (*Seventh-day Adventist Bible Dictionary*, p. 569, par. 3; p. 827, par. 3–5).

If Christ was crucified in A.D. 31 (see *Seventh-day Adventist Bible Dictionary*, p. 569), and Paul kept the feast of Passover and Unleavened Bread in spring A.D. 57, then Paul did so 26 years after the crucifixion.

The Seventh-day Adventist Bible Dictionary states on page 853: "In *no place* did Paul reprove the Philippians for moral corruption or *erroneous doctrines*."

"Brethren, be followers ["co-imitators," G4831] together of me, and mark them which walk so as *ye have us for an ensample*" (Phil. 3:17).

"Those things, which ye have both learned, and received, and heard, and seen in me, do: and the God of peace shall be with you" (Phil. 4:9).

"You *became followers* ["imitators," G3402] *of us and of the Lord*, for you welcomed the message in the midst of severe suffering with the joy given by the Holy Spirit. And so you became a model to all the believers in Macedonia and Achaia" (1 Thess. 1:6, 7).

"We did this, not because we do not have the right to such help, but in order to offer ourselves as a model for you to follow ["imitate," G3401]" (2 Thess. 3:9).

"Wherefore I beseech you, *be ye followers* ["imitators," G3402] *of me*" (1 Cor. 4:16).

"*Be ye followers* ["imitators," G3402] *of me, even as I also am of Christ*" (1 Cor. 11:1).

"Whereunto I am ordained a preacher, and an apostle, (I speak the truth in Christ, and lie not;) a teacher of the Gentiles in faith and verity" (1 Tim. 2:7).

"I say the truth in Christ, I lie not, my conscience also bearing me witness in the Holy Ghost" (Rom. 9:1).

"Now the things which I write unto you, behold, before God, I lie not" (Gal. 1:20).

Note: The rejection of Paul's example to the Philippians is one of the doctrines that Protestant churches, unfortunately, still share with Catholicism, in spite of the above separate statements to the Philippian, Thessalonian, and Corinthian churches, and Luke's documentation of Paul's keeping of the statutes in Acts, chapter 20.

"Therefore let us keep the feast, not with old leaven, neither with the leaven of malice and wickedness; but with the unleavened bread of sincerity and *truth* [G225]" (1 Cor. 5:8).

" 'Brethren, we are now erelong to part asunder, and the Lord knoweth whether I shall live ever to see your faces more. But whether the Lord hath appointed it or not, I charge you before God and His blessed angels to follow me no farther than I have followed Christ. If God should reveal anything to you by any other instrument of His, be as ready to receive it as ever you were to receive any truth of my ministry; for I am very confident the Lord hath more truth and light yet to break forth out of His holy word.'—Martyn 5:70" (GC 291.4).

James

"But if ye have respect to persons, ye commit sin, and are convinced of the law as transgressors" (James 2:9).

"Ye shall do no unrighteousness in judgment: thou shalt not respect the person of the poor, nor honor the person of the mighty: but in righteousness shalt thou judge thy neighbour" (Lev. 19:15).

Jude

"Even as Sodom and Gomorrha, and the cities about them in like manner, giving themselves over to fornication [Deut. 22:13–21], and going after strange flesh, are set forth for an example, suffering the vengeance of eternal fire" (Jude 7).

John

"Blessed are they that do his commandments, that they may have right to the tree of life, and may enter in through the gates into the city. For without are dogs, and sorcerers [Deut. 18:10; Exod. 22:18], and whoremongers [Lev. 21:7, 9], and murderers, and idolaters, and whosoever loveth and maketh a lie [Lev. 6:1–5; 19:12]" (Rev. 22:14, 15).

CHAPTER 7

WHAT WAS *NOT* NAILED TO THE CROSS

This is a chapter I did not want to write. However, because much has been said by supposed theologians in defense of the Catholic position, this becomes necessary to remind people and show them that Scripture and the law have not been changed.

Jesus stated: "Think not that I am come to destroy the law, or the prophets: I am not come to destroy, but to fulfil" (Matt. 5:17). This means exactly what it says. What was fulfilled? The temple service, the sacrifices, the priesthood, circumcision, other bloodletting in the temple, and the offerings made by fire.

"… Christ also hath loved us, and hath given himself for us an offering and a sacrifice to God for a sweetsmelling savour" (Eph. 5:2). This is a fulfillment of Daniel 9:27: "… in the midst of the week he shall cause the sacrifice ["slaughter," H2077] and the oblation ["meat offering," H4503] to cease" (Dan. 9:27).

Was there to be a change in the law? Yes, the ceremonial law relating to temple worship was changed, particularly the priesthood. In Hebrews 7:12, Paul, in speaking of the priesthood, states: "For the priesthood being changed, there is made of necessity a change also of the law [*nomos*, G3551]." What law is Paul calling *nomos*? The ceremonial law!

Yet, theologians claim that Paul calls the entire Mosaic Law *dogma* in Colossians 2. This is an example of what Peter warned us of in 2 Peter 3:16: "As also in all his epistles, speaking in them of these things; in which are some things hard to be understood, which they that are unlearned and unstable wrest, as they do also the other scriptures, unto their own destruction."

Since the days of Christ, intelligent men have been making excuses for why they don't believe. The Pharisees said to the officers, "Are ye also deceived? Have any of the rulers or of the Pharisees believed on him? ... Art thou also of Galilee? Search, and look: for out of Galilee ariseth no prophet" (John 7:47, 48, 52).

Now, the above statement is true. The Pharisees had not accepted Christ, and no prophet had been prophesied to come from Galilee. However, it was a conclusion that they had come to by the most superficial study of Christ's origins. You see, they did not want to know the truth. If we look in Scripture to find what we want, we can wind up like many theologians who read a lot of things into Scripture.

Paul's reference to the Sabbath in Colossians, chapter 2, is significant. Sabbath-keepers who do not wish to keep the feasts say that Paul repeats himself in the items in verse 16. Paul says, "Let no man therefore judge you in meat, or in drink, or in respect of an holyday ["feast," G1859], or of the new moon, or of the Sabbath ["the Lord's Sabbath," G4521, from H7676] days" (Col. 2:16). Paul *does not say*, let no man therefore judge you in meat or drink or in respect of a feast or of the new moon or of the feast.

Ellen White, in *Patriarchs and Prophets*, states: "Again the people were reminded of the sacred obligation of the Sabbath. Yearly feasts were appointed, at which all the men of the nation were to assemble before the Lord, bringing to Him their offerings of gratitude and the first fruits of His bounties. The object of all these regulations was stated: they proceeded from no exercise of mere arbitrary sovereignty; all were given for the good of Israel. The Lord said, 'Ye shall be holy men unto Me' [Exod. 22:31]—worthy to be acknowledged by a holy God. These laws were to be recorded by Moses, and carefully treasured as the *foundation* of the national law, and, *with* the ten precepts which they were given to illustrate, the condition of the fulfillment of God's promises to Israel" (PP 311.2, 3).

Theologians who state that these appointments in time *were,* instead of *are*, shadows of things to come contradict translations of the King James Version and modern translations, and Ellen G. White who states in *The Great Controversy*: "In like manner the types which relate to the second advent must be fulfilled at the time pointed out in the symbolic service" (GC 399.4).

This effort to support Catholic theology about the appointments of their feasts, changing the *appointed times* while also attacking Catholic theology regarding the Sabbath, is religious schizophrenia at best.

Regarding what was nailed to the cross, *dogma* is not *nomos*. Without adding words and using literal interpretations, this is how Colossians 2:16, 17, reads: "Therefore, no one is to act as your judge in regard to food and drink, or in respect to a festival or a new moon, or a Sabbath day— things which are a shadow of what is to come; but the body of Christ [margin]" (Col. 2:16, 17, *New American Standard Bible)*. This text reads just fine without *added* words or changing words from their literal meaning.

The Sabbath is not connected to the feasts just in the Old Testament but in the New Testament as well.

"All who exalt their own opinions above divine revelation, all who would change the plain meaning of Scripture to suit their own convenience, or for the sake of conforming to the world, are taking upon themselves a fearful responsibility. The written word, the law of God, will measure the character of every man and condemn all whom this unerring test shall declare wanting" (GC 268.2).

"The language of the Bible should be explained according to its obvious meaning, unless a symbol or figure is employed. Christ has given the promise: 'If any man will do His will, he shall know of the doctrine.' John 7:17" (GC 598.3).

"The whole Bible should be given to the people just as it reads" (GC 521.2).

"But God will have a people upon the earth to maintain the Bible, and the Bible only, as the standard of all doctrines and the basis of all reforms" (GC 595.1).

"He [Satan] well knows that the curse of God will rest on those who exalt human enactments above the divine, and he does all in his power to lead men into the broad road that ends in destruction" (PK 186.1).

Regarding Galatians 4:8–11, many use these verses as a rationale for not believing some of the statutes. If they looked more carefully, they would notice that Luke documented Paul's obedience to the statutes they loathe. "Howbeit then, when ye knew not God, ye did service unto them which by nature are no gods" (Gal. 4:8).

Using the Bible to interpret itself, note the following texts:

"Hath a nation changed their gods, which are yet *no gods*? but my people have changed their glory for that which doth not profit" (Jer. 2:11).

"How shall I pardon thee for this? thy children have forsaken me, and sworn by them that are *no gods*: when I had fed them to the full, they then committed adultery, and assembled themselves by troops in the harlots' houses" (Jer. 5:7).

"Shall a man make gods unto himself, and they are *no gods*?" (Jer. 16:20).

"And have cast their gods into the fire: for they were *no gods*, but the work of men's hands, wood and stone: therefore they have destroyed them" (Isa. 37:19).

"Moreover ye see and hear, that not alone at Ephesus, but almost throughout all Asia, this Paul hath persuaded and turned away much people, saying that they be *no gods*, which are made with hands" (Acts 19:26).

"And have cast their gods into the fire: for they were *no gods*, but the work of men's hands, wood and stone: therefore they have destroyed them" (2 Kings 19:18).

"Have ye not cast out the priests of the LORD, the sons of Aaron, and the Levites, and have made you priests after the manner of the nations of other lands? so that whosoever cometh to consecrate himself with a young bullock and seven rams, the same may be a priest of them that are *no gods*" (2 Chron. 13:9).

In every case, "no gods" are used to describe idols, which is exactly what Paul is talking about here when "... ye knew not God" (Gal. 4:8). Paul is speaking of a time when the Galatians were idolaters. "But now, after that ye have known God, or rather are known of God, how turn ye again to the weak and beggarly elements, whereunto ye desire again to be in bondage? Ye observe days, and months, and times, and years" (Gal. 4:9, 10).

What were the pagan elements or rudiments? And, what were those times they were observing? Again, using the Bible to interpret itself, let's examine the following texts:

"Ye shall not eat any thing with the blood: neither shall ye use enchantment, nor *observe times*" (Lev. 19:26).

"There shall not be found among you any one that maketh his son or his daughter to pass through the fire, or that useth divination, or an *observer of times*, or an enchanter, or a witch. For these nations, which thou shalt possess, hearkened unto observers of times, and unto diviners: but as for thee, the LORD thy God hath not suffered thee so to do" (Deut. 18:10, 14).

"And he caused his children to pass through the fire in the valley of the son of Hinnom: also he *observed times*, and used enchantments, and used witchcraft, and dealt with a familiar spirit, and with wizards: he wrought much evil in the sight of the LORD, to provoke him to anger" (2 Chron. 33:6).

"And he made his son pass through the fire, and *observed times*, and used enchantments, and dealt with familiar spirits and wizards: he wrought much wickedness in the sight of the LORD, to provoke him to anger" (2 Kings 21:6).

Note: These Old Testament scriptures that describe people observing "times" are associated with pagan worship.

Now, instead of attacking God's statutes here in Galatians, we see that Paul is upholding and teaching them.

Brothers and sisters, be careful who you listen to. *The Scriptures do not attack other Scriptures.* God has given man the commandments, laws, statutes, judgments and testimonies for his happiness. "Study to shew thyself approved unto God, a workman that needeth not to be ashamed, *rightly* dividing the word of *truth* [G225]" (2 Tim. 2:15).

Be careful of the wolves, who come to you saying that the practices and teachings of Jesus are not required of those who follow in His footsteps.

> "The Scriptures do not attack other Scriptures. God has given man the commandments, laws, statutes, judgments and testimonies for his happiness."

"God has given us His word that we may become acquainted with its teachings and know for ourselves what He requires of us. When the lawyer came to Jesus with the inquiry, 'What shall I do to inherit eternal life?' the Saviour referred him to the Scriptures, saying: 'What is written in the law? how readest thou?' Ignorance will not excuse young or old, nor release them from the punishment due for the transgression of God's law; because there is in their hands a faithful presentation of that law and of its principles and claims. It is not enough to have good intentions; it is not enough to do what a man thinks is right or what the minister tells him is right. His soul's salvation is at stake, and he should search the Scriptures for himself. However strong may be his convictions, however confident he may be that the minister knows what is truth, this is not his foundation. He has a chart pointing out every waymark on the heavenward journey, and he ought not to guess at anything" (GC 598.1).

"Many a portion of Scripture which learned men pronounce a mystery, or pass over as unimportant, is full of comfort and instruction to him who has been taught in the school of Christ. *One reason why many theologians have no clearer understanding of God's word is, they close their eyes to truths which they do not wish to practice. An understanding of Bible truth depends not so much on the power of intellect brought to the search as on the singleness of purpose, the earnest longing after righteousness"* (GC 599.2).

Regarding Colossians 2:14

Pastors have stood in the pulpit and preached that, because the law of Moses was written in a book, it was only temporary, while the ten precepts are lasting because they were written by the finger of God in stone! Do they mean the law spoken of in Deuteronomy 28:58–62, where it says "If thou wilt not observe to do *all* the words of this law that are *written* in this *book* ["writing," H5612], that thou mayest fear this glorious and fearful name, *THE LORD THY GOD*; then the LORD will make thy *plagues* wonderful, and the *plagues* of thy seed, even great *plagues*, and of long continuance, and sore sicknesses, and of long continuance. Moreover he will bring upon thee all the diseases of Egypt, which thou wast afraid of; and they shall cleave unto thee. Also every sickness, and every *plague*, which is *not* written in the book of this law [see Rev. 16:1–21], them will the LORD bring upon thee, until thou be destroyed. And ye shall be left few in number, whereas ye were as the stars of heaven for multitude; because thou wouldest not obey the *voice of the LORD thy God"* (Deut. 28:58–62).

Note: The law mentioned above includes the statutes (see Deut. 28:15, 45, and 58).

CHAPTER 8

THE COST OF NOT KEEPING THE COMMANDMENTS, STATUTES, AND JUDGMENTS

The Last Thing David Told Solomon

"And keep the charge of the LORD thy God, to walk in his ways, to keep his *statutes, and* his *commandments, and* his *judgments, and* his *testimonies,* as it is *written in the law of Moses,* that thou mayest prosper in all that thou doest, and whithersoever thou turnest thyself" (1 Kings 2:3).

David's Prayer for Solomon

"And give unto Solomon my son a perfect heart, to keep thy *commandments,* thy *testimonies, and* thy *statutes,* and to do all these things, and to build the palace, for the which I have made provision" (1 Chron. 29:19).

God's Promise to Solomon

" And if thou wilt walk before me, as David thy father walked, in integrity of heart, and in uprightness, to do according to all that I have commanded thee, and wilt keep my *statutes and* my *judgments*: then I will establish the throne of thy kingdom upon Israel for ever ... But if ye shall at all turn from following me, ye or your children, and will not keep my *commandments and* my *statutes* which I have set before you, but go and serve other gods, and worship them: then will I cut off Israel out of the land which I have given them; and this house, which I have hallowed for my name, will I cast out of my sight; and Israel shall be a proverb and a byword among all people" (1 Kings 9:4–7).

"And as for thee, if thou wilt walk before me, as David thy father walked, and do according to all that I have commanded thee, and shalt observe my *statutes and* my *judgments*; then will I stablish the throne of thy kingdom, according as I have covenanted with David thy father, saying, There shall not fail thee a man to be ruler in Israel. But if ye turn away, and forsake my *statutes and* my *commandments*, which I have set before you, and shall go and serve other gods, and worship them; then will I pluck them up by the roots out of my land which I have given them" (2 Chron. 7:17–20).

Why Solomon Lost the Ten Tribes

"And he said to Jeroboam, Take thee ten pieces: for thus saith the LORD, the God of Israel, Behold, I will rend the kingdom out of the hand of Solomon, and will give ten tribes to thee: (But he shall have one tribe for my servant David's sake, and for Jerusalem's sake, the city which I have chosen out of all the tribes of Israel:) Because that they have forsaken me, and have worshipped Ashtoreth the goddess of the Zidonians, Chemosh the god of the Moabites, and Milcom the god of the children of Ammon, and have *not walked in my ways*, to do that which is right in mine eyes, and to keep my *statutes and* my *judgments*, as did David his father. Howbeit I will not take the whole kingdom out of his hand: but I will make him prince all the days of his life for David my servant's sake, whom I chose, *because he kept my commandments and my statutes*" (1 Kings 11:31–34).

God's Promise to Jeroboam

Jeroboam Was Offered the Same Deal.

"And it shall be, if thou wilt hearken unto all that I command thee, and wilt walk in my ways, and do that is right in my sight, to keep my *statutes and* my *commandments*, as David my servant did; that I will be with thee, and build thee a sure house, as I built for David, and will give Israel unto thee" (1 Kings 11:38).

CHAPTER 9

THE SINS OF JEROBOAM

The sins of Jeroboam included his attempted change of God's *moeds*. These sins are documented in Scripture and remembered by God in the ultimate judgment of Israel.

"And it shall be, if thou wilt hearken unto all that I command thee, and wilt walk in my ways, and do that is right in my sight, to keep my *statutes* and my *commandments*, as David my servant did; that I will be with thee, and build thee a sure house, as I built for David, and will give Israel unto thee." *However*, "Jeroboam ordained a feast in the eighth month, on the fifteenth day of the month, like unto the feast that is in Judah, and he offered upon the altar. So did he in Bethel, sacrificing unto the calves that he had made: and he placed in Bethel the priests of the high places which he had made. So he offered upon the altar which he had made in Bethel the fifteenth day of the eighth month, even in the month which he had devised of his own heart; and ordained a feast unto the children of Israel: and he offered upon the altar, and burnt incense" (1 Kings 11:38; 12:32, 33).

"And he shall give Israel up because of the sins of Jeroboam, who did sin, and who made Israel to sin" (1 Kings 14:16).

The Catholic Church is the antitype of the Northern Kingdom.

A. Like Israel, it apostatized.
B. Like Jeroboam, it changed the priesthood and the feast times and introduced idolatry.
C. Like Israel, its sins were continual for generations.

For 241½ years, nineteen kings led their people in the "sins of Jeroboam" until the end of the kingdom. These kings are listed with their sins in the following texts:

King Nadab – 1 Kings 15:25, 26.
King Baasha – 1 Kings 15:33, 34.
King Elah – 1 Kings 16:6, 7.
King Zimri – 1 Kings 16:18, 19.
King Omri – 1 Kings 16:25, 26.
King Ahab – 1 Kings 16:30, 31.
King Ahaziah – 1 Kings 22:51, 52.
King Jehoram – 2 Kings 3:1–3.
King Jehu – 2 Kings 10:28, 29.
King Jehoahaz – 2 Kings 13:1, 2.
King Jehoash – 2 Kings 13:10, 11.
King Jeroboam (son of Jehoash) – 2 Kings 14:23, 24.
King Zachariah – 2 Kings 15:8, 9.
King Shallum – 2 Kings 15:13, 14. (He is the only king of Israel of whom God does not say he continued in the sins of Jeroboam—probably because he only reigned for one month.)
King Menahem – 2 Kings 15:17, 18.
King Pekahiah – 2 Kings 15:23, 24.
King Pekah – 2 Kings 15:27, 28.
King Hoshea – 2 Kings 15:30; 17:4, 22, 23.

The results of the sins of Jeroboam are found in 2 Kings 17:6–8, 13, 14, including: *"Yet the LORD testified against Israel, and against Judah, by all the prophets, and by all the seers, saying, Turn ye from your evil ways, and keep my commandments and my statutes, according to all the law which I commanded your fathers, and which I sent to you by my servants the prophets. Notwithstanding they would not hear, but hardened their necks, like to the neck of their fathers, that did not believe in the LORD their God. ... For the children of Israel walked in all the sins of Jeroboam which he did; they departed not from them; until the LORD removed Israel out of his sight, as he had said by all his servants the prophets.* So was Israel carried away out of their own land to Assyria unto this day" (2 Kings 17:13, 14, 22, 23).

"And the king of Assyria did carry away Israel unto Assyria, and put them in Halah and in Habor by the river of Gozan, and in the cities of the Medes: because they obeyed not the voice of the LORD their God, *but transgressed his covenant, and all that Moses the servant of the LORD commanded*, and would not hear them, nor do them" (2 Kings 18:11, 12).

In the closing days of the northern kingdom, God gave Israel a last chance. "A Passover celebration was arranged for, and to this feast were invited not only the tribes of Judah and Benjamin, over which Hezekiah had been anointed king, but all the northern tribes as well. A proclamation was sounded 'throughout all Israel, from Beersheba even to Dan, that they should come to keep the Passover unto the Lord God of Israel at Jerusalem: for they had not done it of a long time in such sort as it was written' " (PK 287.3).

"But the remnant of the ten tribes still dwelling within the territory of the once-flourishing northern kingdom treated the royal messengers from Judah with indifference and even with contempt.... About two years later, Samaria was invested by the hosts of Assyria under Shalmaneser; and in the siege that followed, multitudes perished miserably of hunger and disease as well as by the sword. The city and nation fell, and the broken remnant of the ten tribes were carried away captive and scattered in the provinces of the Assyrian realm. *The destruction that befell the northern kingdom was a direct judgment from Heaven*" (PK 291.1–3).

"The king's bold defiance of God in thus setting aside *divinely appointed institutions* was not allowed to pass unrebuked" (PK 101.3).

"Grievously had the children of Israel 'sinned against the Lord their God, . . . and wrought wicked things.' 'They would not hear, but . . . rejected His *statutes*, and His *covenant* that He made with their fathers, and His testimonies which He testified against them.' ... 'So was Israel carried away out of their own land to Assyria,' 'because they obeyed not the voice of the Lord their God, but *transgressed His covenant*, and *all that Moses the servant of the Lord commanded.*' 2 Kings 17:7, 11, 14–16, 20, 23; 18:12" (PK 291.4–292.1).

> "If God kept track of the sins of a group of people for 241 years and then, ultimately, destroyed them for those sins, shouldn't we be careful not to follow in these same sins?"

Notes:

1. If God kept track of the sins of a group of people for 241 years and then, ultimately, destroyed them for those sins, shouldn't we be careful not to follow in these same sins?
2. How were they and how are we to keep the statutes and commandments? "Forevermore" (2 Kings 17:37).

CHAPTER 10

THE ELIJAH MESSAGE

The conditions given for the early and latter rains—both literal and spiritual—God had given to Israel through Moses.

"Therefore thou shalt *love the LORD thy God*, and *keep his charge*, and *his statutes*, and *his judgments*, and *his commandments*, alway. And it shall come to pass, if ye shall hearken diligently unto my commandments which I command you this day, to love the LORD your God, and to serve him with all your heart and with all your soul, that I will give you the rain of your land in his due season, the first rain and the latter rain, that thou mayest gather in thy corn, and thy wine, and thine oil. Therefore shall ye lay up these my words in your heart and in your soul, and bind them for a sign upon your hand, that they may be as frontlets between your eyes. And ye shall teach them your children, speaking of them when thou sittest in thine house, and when thou walkest by the way, when thou liest down, and when thou risest up. For if ye shall diligently keep all these commandments which I command you, to do them, to love the LORD your God, to walk in all his ways, and to cleave unto him; then will the LORD drive out all these nations from before you, and ye shall possess greater nations and mightier than yourselves. Every place whereon the soles of your feet shall tread shall be yours: from the wilderness and Lebanon, from the river, the river Euphrates, even unto the uttermost sea shall your coast be. *There shall no man be able to stand before you*: for the LORD your God shall lay the fear of you and the dread of you upon all the land that ye shall tread upon, as he hath said unto you. And ye shall observe to do all the statutes and judgments which I set before you this day. Therefore shall ye keep all the commandments which I command you this day, that ye may be strong, and go in and possess the land, whither ye go to possess it; and that ye may prolong your days in the land, which the LORD sware unto your fathers to give unto them and to their seed, a land that floweth with milk and honey" (Deut. 11:1, 13, 14, 18, 19, 22–25, 32, 8, 9).

"Plain were these commands, yet as the centuries passed, and generation after generation lost sight of the *provision made for their spiritual welfare*, the ruinous influences of apostasy threatened to sweep aside every barrier of divine grace" (PK 136.3).

Regarding Elijah and his message, at this time, Ellen White states: "He [God] had delivered them from bondage and given them 'the lands of the heathen, ...*that they might observe His statutes, and keep His laws.*' Psalm 105:44, 45" (PK 119.2).

It was into the time, after the split of the kingdoms and the national apostasy of Israel, that God sent Elijah to rebuke the syncretistic worship of the Northern kingdom.

There were three false teachings that made up the sins of Jeroboam.

1. "In this effort to represent the Deity, Jeroboam violated the plain command of Jehovah: 'Thou shalt not make unto thee any graven image.... Thou shalt not bow down thyself to them, nor serve them.' Exodus 20:4, 5" (PK 100.1).
2. "He was therefore compelled to elevate to the priesthood men from 'the lowest of the people.' [1 Kings 12:31]" (PK 101.1).
3. " 'Jeroboam ordained a feast in the eighth month, on the fifteenth day of the month, like unto the feast that is in Judah, and he offered upon the altar. So did he in Bethel, sacrificing unto the calves that he had made: and he placed in Bethel the priests of the high places which he had made.' [1 Kings 12:32]" (PK 101.2).

"The king's bold defiance of God in thus setting aside *divinely appointed institutions* was not allowed to pass unrebuked" (PK 101.3).

"The prevailing spirit of our time is one of infidelity and apostasy—a spirit of avowed illumination because of a knowledge of truth, but in reality of the blindest presumption. Human theories are exalted and placed where God and His law should be. There is seen a spirit of opposition to the plain word of God, of idolatrous exaltation of human wisdom above divine revelation. Men have allowed their minds to become so darkened and confused by conformity to worldly customs and influences that they seem to have lost all power to discriminate between light and darkness, truth and error. ... A faith such as actuated Paul, Peter, and John they regard as old-fashioned, mystical, and unworthy of the intelligence of modern thinkers.

"In the beginning, God gave His law to mankind as a means of attaining happiness and eternal life. Satan's only hope of thwarting the purpose of God is to lead men and women to disobey this law, and his constant effort has been to misrepresent its teachings and belittle its importance. *His master stroke has been an attempt to change the law itself, so as to lead men to violate its precepts while professing to obey it*" (PK 178.1–2).

The Elijah message to come is pictured in Malachi: "*Remember ye the law of Moses my servant*, which I commanded unto him in Horeb for all Israel, with the statutes and judgments. Behold, I will send you Elijah the prophet before the coming of the great and dreadful day of the LORD: and he shall turn the heart of the fathers to the children, and the heart of the children to their fathers, lest I come and smite the earth with a curse" (Mal. 4:4–6).

"That the obligations of the Decalogue might be more fully understood and enforced, additional precepts were given, illustrating and applying the principles of the Ten Commandments. These laws were called judgments, both because they were framed in infinite wisdom and equity and because the magistrates were to give judgment according to them. Unlike the Ten Commandments, they were delivered privately to Moses, who was to communicate them to the people" (PP 310.1).

"It is only as the law of God is restored to its rightful position that there can be a revival of primitive faith and godliness among His professed people. 'Thus saith the Lord, Stand ye in the ways, and see, and ask for the old paths, where is the good way, and walk therein, and ye shall find rest for your souls.' Jeremiah 6:16" (GC 478.3).

> "It is only as the law of God is restored to its rightful position that there can be a revival of primitive faith and godliness among His professed people."

"The whole Bible should be given to the people just as it reads" (GC 521; see also GC 268.2; 595.1; 598.3; PK 178.1; 185.2; 5T 171).

"In His word, God has committed to men the knowledge necessary for salvation. The *Holy Scriptures are to be accepted as an authoritative, infallible revelation of His will. They are the standard of character, the revealer of doctrines, and the test of experience.* 'Every scripture inspired of God is also *profitable for teaching, for reproof, for correction, for instruction* which is in righteousness; that the man of

God may be complete, furnished completely unto every good work.' 2 Timothy 3:16, 17, Revised Version" (GC vii.1).

"What was the origin of the great apostasy? How did the church first depart from the simplicity of the gospel? By conforming to the practices of paganism, to facilitate the acceptance of Christianity by the heathen" (GC 384.5).

This is syncretism, and, while its most blatant forms—the mass, transubstantiation and purgatory—have been rejected by most of the Protestant world, there are still vestiges remaining. The sunrise worship, eggs and bunnies of pagan Easter, pagan totems of Christmas, and the acceptance of the dates of these pagan holidays as still relevant to the Christian religion.

God then as now wants His people to come away from these pagan religious ceremonies. Because of the length of time these practices have been in the church and because their parents and grandparents believed and worshiped this way, people are reluctant to give them up.

Worse than this is the setting aside of God's statutes and judgments as part of the moral law. The idea that these are not a tenable part of His moral law goes back 1700 years.

These were the changes by Catholicism in the 4th century, which are still accepted by most of the Protestant world and those who define themselves as part of the remnant church of Revelation.

"There are many at the present day thus clinging to the customs and traditions of their fathers. When the Lord sends them additional light, they refuse to accept it, because, not having been granted to their fathers, it was not received by them. We are not placed where our fathers were; consequently our duties and responsibilities are not the same as theirs. We shall not be approved of God in looking to the example of our fathers to determine our duty instead of searching the word of truth for ourselves. *Our responsibility is greater than was that of our ancestors*. We are accountable for the light which they received, and which was handed down as an inheritance for us, and we are accountable also for the additional light which is now shining upon us from the word of God" (GC 164.1).

"Let none deceive themselves with the belief that they can become holy while willfully violating *one* of God's requirements. The *commission of a known sin silences the witnessing voice of the Spirit and separates the soul from God*. If men feel no weight of the *moral law, if they belittle and make light of God's precepts*, if they break *one* of the *least* of these commandments, and teach men so, they shall be of no esteem in the sight of Heaven ..." (GC 472.3).

Elijah was the type for John the Baptist and the end-time Elijah, who were and are to call people back to the true worship of their Father; denouncing the commandments of men and teaching the law of God. Just as the Holy Spirit calls men to *righteousness*—the keeping of God's law—and away from *sin*—the transgression of God's law—and *judgment*—the results of rejecting the law of God, the end-time Elijah will present one last opportunity for salvation (see John 16:8).

"From the very beginning of the great controversy in heaven it has been Satan's purpose to overthrow the law of God. It was to accomplish this that he entered upon his rebellion against the Creator, and though he was cast out of heaven he has continued the same warfare upon the earth. To deceive men, and thus lead them to transgress God's law, is the object which he has steadfastly pursued. Whether this be accomplished by casting aside the law altogether, or by rejecting one of its precepts, the result will be ultimately the same. He that offends 'in one point,' manifests contempt for the whole law; his influence and example are on the side of transgression; he becomes 'guilty of all.' James 2:10.

"In seeking to cast contempt upon the divine statutes, Satan has perverted the doctrines of the Bible, and errors have thus become incorporated into the faith of thousands who profess to believe the Scriptures. The last great conflict between truth and error is but the final struggle of the long-standing controversy concerning the law of God. Upon this battle we are now entering—a battle between the laws of men and the precepts of Jehovah, between the religion of the Bible and the religion of fable and tradition" (GC 582.2).

"When the Saviour pointed out to His followers the signs of His return, He foretold the state of backsliding that would exist just prior to His second advent. There would be, as in the days of Noah, the activity and stir of worldly business and pleasure seeking—buying, selling, planting, building, marrying, and giving in marriage—with forgetfulness of God and the future life. For those living at this time, Christ's admonition is: 'Take heed to yourselves, lest at any time your hearts be overcharged with surfeiting, and drunkenness, and cares of this life, and so that day come upon you unawares.' 'Watch ye therefore, and pray always, that ye may be accounted worthy to escape all these things that shall come to pass, and to stand before the Son of man.' Luke 21:34, 36" (GC 309.2).

The results of rejecting God's law are seen in the history of the northern kingdom. The hardening of the hearts of those rejecters of God's message and law was typical of that which will occur at the end of time when Elijah comes again. In a last plea for God's children to return to the Father, they will receive the final call. Like the people in the days of Noah, the children of Lot, and the tribes of the northern kingdom, they won't know when the last message of mercy is being presented.

"In view of that great day the word of God, in the most solemn and impressive language, calls upon His people to arouse from their spiritual lethargy and to seek His face with repentance and humiliation: 'Blow ye the trumpet in Zion, and sound an alarm in My holy mountain: let all the inhabitants of the land tremble: for the day of the Lord cometh, for it is nigh at hand.' 'Sanctify a fast, call a solemn assembly: gather the people, sanctify the congregation, assemble the elders, gather the children: ... let the bridegroom go forth of his chamber, and the bride out of her closet. Let the priests, the ministers of the Lord, weep between the porch and the altar.' 'Turn ye even to Me with all your heart, and with fasting, and with weeping, and with mourning: and rend your heart, and not your garments, and turn unto the Lord your God: for He is gracious and merciful, slow to anger, and of great kindness.' Joel 2:1, 15–17, 12, 13.

"To prepare a people to stand in the day of God, *a great work of reform* was to be accomplished. God saw that many of His professed people were not building for eternity, and in His mercy He was about to send a message of warning to arouse them from their stupor and lead them to make ready for the coming of the Lord.

"This warning is brought to view in Revelation 14. Here is a threefold message represented as proclaimed by heavenly beings and immediately followed by the coming of the Son of man to reap 'the harvest of the earth.' The first of these warnings announces the approaching judgment. The prophet beheld an angel flying 'in the midst of heaven, having the everlasting gospel to preach unto them that dwell on the earth, and to every nation, and kindred, and tongue, and people, saying with a loud voice, Fear God, and give glory to Him; for the hour of His judgment is come: and worship Him that made heaven, and earth, and the sea, and the fountains of waters.' Revelation 14:6, 7" (GC 311.1–3).

CHAPTER 11

THE FEASTS

"Christ passed through all the experiences of His childhood, youth, and manhood without the observance of *ceremonial temple worship*" (*Bible Echo*, Oct. 31, 1898, par. 7).

Note: Jesus never kept the ceremonial law, but He did keep the feasts.

"Among the Jews the twelfth year was the dividing line between childhood and youth. On completing this year a Hebrew boy was called a son of the law, and also a son of God. He was given special opportunities for religious instruction, and was expected to participate in the sacred feasts and observances. It was in accordance with this custom that Jesus in His boyhood made the Passover visit to Jerusalem" (DA 75.1).

During His ministry, "Jesus traveled up and down the breadth of the land, giving his invitation to the feast. When the sun illuminated the landscape, Jesus said to the vast throng: 'I am the light of the world: he that followeth me shall not walk in darkness, but shall have the light of life.' He took the opportunity of presenting himself to the people during the feast-days, when they gathered at Jerusalem" (*Review and Herald*, July 7, 1896, par. 2).

"There were three annual feasts, the Passover, the Pentecost, and the Feast of Tabernacles, at which all the men of Israel were commanded to appear before the Lord at Jerusalem. Of these feasts the Passover was the most largely attended. Many were present from all countries where the Jews were scattered. From every part of Palestine the worshipers came in great numbers. The journey from Galilee occupied several days, and the travelers united in large companies for companionship and protection. The women and aged men rode upon oxen or asses over the steep and rocky roads. The stronger men and the youth journeyed on foot. The time of the Passover corresponded to the close of March or the beginning of April, and the whole land was bright with flowers, and glad with the song of birds. All along the way were spots memorable in the history of Israel, and fathers and mothers recounted to their children the wonders that God had wrought for His people in ages past. They beguiled their journey with song and music, and when at last the towers of Jerusalem came into view, every voice joined in the triumphant strain" (DA 75.2).

"All the world are invited to come to the gospel feast. Jesus has called all sinners to himself. 'Many are called, but few are chosen.' The voice of entreaty comes to the careless and the impenitent, saying, 'Turn ye, turn ye from your evil ways; for why will ye die?' The Lord has sent forth his entreating invitation. ..." (Review and Herald, July 7, 1896, par. 1).

[Jesus] took the opportunity of presenting himself to the people during the feast-days, when they gathered at Jerusalem. The people met together to carry out the instructions given to Moses, to 'observe the feast of tabernacles seven days, after that thou hast gathered in thy corn and thy wine;' and *Jesus himself stood in the midst of them*. The feast of tabernacles was the great holiday of the nation. This feast was preceded by a day of atonement, which occurred on the tenth day of the seventh month, when every one was to afflict his soul by confessing his sins, both to the Lord and to his brethren. This humiliation was to prepare the way for the celebration of the feast of tabernacles, which lasted seven days, and was a memorial of the protecting care of God when he led Israel through the wilderness. In the instruction to Moses, he said: 'Also in the fifteenth day of the seventh month, when ye have gathered in the fruit of the land, ye shall keep a feast unto the Lord seven days: on the first day shall be a sabbath, and on the eighth day shall be a sabbath. And ye shall take you on the first day the boughs of goodly trees, branches of palm-trees, and the boughs of thick trees, and willows of the brook; and ye shall rejoice before the Lord your God seven days. And ye shall keep it a feast unto the Lord seven days in the year. It shall be a statute forever in your generations: ye shall celebrate it in the seventh month. Ye shall dwell in booths seven days; all that are Israelites born shall dwell in booths: that your generations may know that I made the children of Israel to dwell in booths, when I brought them out of the land of Egypt: I am the Lord your God.' [Leviticus 23:40–43.] It was to the celebration of this feast that Jesus came. ...

"... He directed them to search the Scriptures; for it was essential that they should interpret correctly the mission and work of the Son of God. ... His life was the light of men, and he presented his life before the people, that their faith might lay hold upon it, and that they might become one with him.

"Though he presented infinite truth, *he left many things unsaid that he might have said*, because even his disciples were not able to comprehend them. He said, 'I have yet many things to say unto you, but ye cannot bear them now.' [John 16:12.] The *burden of his teaching* was *obedience to* the *commandments of God*, that would work transformation of character and inculcate moral excellence, shaping the soul after the divine similitude. Christ had been sent to earth to represent God in character. ...

"... *The principles which he expounded were announced to Moses* from the pillar of cloud, and to the prophets, who spoke and wrote as they were moved upon by the Holy Spirit. ...

"He who fully purposes is his heart to do the will of God, at whatever self-denial or self- sacrifice, will certainly know the truth through his own experience. Those who will obey God's commandments, and not deviate from the precepts of Heaven, will enter into life. *To will to do the will of God, is to yield the whole mind and affections to the control of God*. Such a one will know of the doctrine, not be in questioning and doubt, not be halting between two opinions; *for he will be willing to submit all to God*, realizing that he has purchased all. It is when we give ourselves to Christ, to do his will, that we realize the truth of the saying of David, 'The entrance of thy words giveth light; it giveth understanding unto the simple.' [Psalm 119:130.] It is then that reason and conscience are fully in harmony with the will of God, and there is no collision between the truth of God and the soul.

"The *doctrines* that *Christ taught* are essential for the salvation of the soul; for perfection of character is the result of *willing obedience to the truth as it is in Jesus*. This is the faith that works by love and purifies the soul. ...

"If the Jewish nation had accepted the light that Christ brought to them, it would have revealed to them their need of a Saviour, their need of atonement, their need of the purifying, pardoning love of God. It would have revealed to them the *significance* of the atonement which they had been celebrating, and *fitted them to enjoy the feast of tabernacles* and to rejoice before the Lord. They would have realized that God does not require simply a portion of the heart; but that acceptable service to himself means the consecration of heart, mind, soul, and strength. ..." (*Review and Herald*, July 7, 1896, pars. 2, 4–9).

"The Feast of Tabernacles was *not only commemorative but typical*. It not only pointed back to the wilderness sojourn, but, as the feast of harvest, it celebrated the ingathering of the fruits of the earth, and pointed *forward* to the great day of final ingathering, when the Lord of the harvest shall send forth His reapers to gather the tares together in bundles for the fire, and to gather the wheat into His garner. At that time the wicked will all be destroyed. They will become 'as though they had not been.' Obadiah 16" (PP 541.2).

> "For even hereunto were ye called: because Christ also suffered for us, leaving us an example, that ye should follow his steps: who did no sin, neither was guile found in his mouth (1 Peter 2:21, 22)."

Note: The wicked are destroyed at the time of the Feast of Tabernacles.

Christ attended the Feast of Tabernacles, as recorded in the following passages: John 7:1–53, DA 447–454, 485; MH 86; PP 412.

"For even hereunto were ye called: because Christ also suffered for us, leaving us an example, that ye should *follow his steps*: who did no sin, neither was guile found in his mouth" (1 Peter 2:21, 22).

What are *Moeds*?

Moed (H4150). An appointment that is a fixed time, season or festival; a set time or place; an appointed time or place.

1. "And God said, Let there be lights in the firmament of the heaven to divide the day from the night; and let them be for signs, and for *seasons* [H4150], and for days, and years" (Gen. 1:14).
   Note: *Moeds* were one reason the sun and moon were created.
2. "And he said, Behold, I will make thee know what shall be in the last end of the indignation: for at the *time appointed* [H4150] the end shall be" (Dan. 8:19).
   Note: The end of time is a *moed*.
3. God calls the tabernacle in the wilderness, the tabernacle of the "congregation" [*moed*, "appointed time" or "meeting place," H4150] 127 times.
4. "For thou hast said in thine heart, I will ascend into heaven, I will exalt my throne above the stars of God: I will sit also upon the mount of the congregation [*moed*, "appointed time," H4150]" (Isa. 14:13).
   Note: The dwelling place of God is the mount of the *moed* and *Satan wants to replace God there.*

5. "For I know that thou wilt bring me to death, and to the house *appointed* [H4150] for all living" (Job 30:23).
   Note: Our death is a *moed*.
6. "But thou, O LORD, shall endure for ever; and thy remembrance unto all generations. Thou shalt arise, and have mercy upon Zion: for the time to favour her, yea, *the set time* [H4150], is come" (Ps. 102:12, 13).
   Note: *Moeds* are for mercy and favor for all generations.
7. Armageddon can be understood on the basis of its use in Isaiah 14:13, as stated in #4 above.
   Note: *Har-moed* is used in terms of the great contest between Christ and Satan (see *Seventh-day Adventist Bible Commentary*, vol. 7, p. 846). In view of the other *moeds* in scripture, maybe this is wise!
8. "And the LORD spake unto Moses, saying, Speak unto the children of Israel, and say unto them, Concerning the feasts of the LORD, which ye shall proclaim to be holy convocations, even these are my feasts. Six days shall work be done: but the seventh day is the sabbath of rest, an holy convocation; ye shall do no work therein: it is the sabbath of the LORD in all your dwellings. These are the feasts of the LORD, even holy convocations, which ye shall proclaim in their seasons" (Lev. 23:1–4).
   Note: All feasts are *moeds*, including Sabbath; but not all *moeds* are feasts.

There are many more *moeds* in Scripture upon which God intervened in the affairs of men, and delivered His people in miraculous ways; in battle, through divine intervention, at historically momentous births, etc. God will continue to use these times to increase our faith.

Now, I imagine many of you who have read Ellen G. White's book, *The Desire of Ages*, are shouting that, on page 652, she says: "Christ was standing at the point of transition between two economies and their two great festivals. He, the spotless Lamb of God, was about to present Himself as a sin offering, that He would thus bring to an end the system of types and ceremonies that for four thousand years had *pointed to His death*. As He *ate the Passover* with His disciples, He *instituted in its place* the service that was to be the memorial of His great sacrifice. *The* national festival of the Jews was to pass away forever. The *service* which Christ established was to be observed by His followers in all lands and through *all* ages" (DA 652.2).

Note: She does not state that the feasts were all done away with, only that a service was instituted *in the place of Passover*.

"These types were fulfilled, not only as to the event, but as to the time. On the fourteenth day of the first Jewish month, the very day and month on which for fifteen long centuries the Passover lamb had been slain, *Christ*, having eaten the Passover with His disciples, *instituted that feast* which was to commemorate His own death as 'the Lamb of God, which taketh away the sin of the world.' That same night He was taken by wicked hands to be crucified and slain. And as the antitype of the *wave sheaf* our Lord was raised from the dead on the third day, 'the *first fruits* of them that slept,' a sample of all the resurrected just, whose 'vile body' shall be changed, and 'fashioned like unto His glorious body.' verse 20; Philippians 3:21" (GC 399.3).

Note: Did Christ do away with Passover, or did He establish it? He did both, and it was called Passover until it was changed at the First Council of Nicaea in 325.

In *The Great Controversy*, Ellen White states: "The slaying of the *Passover lamb* was a shadow of the death of Christ. Says Paul: 'Christ our Passover is sacrificed for us.' 1 Corinthians 5:7. The sheaf of first fruits, which at the time of the Passover was waved before the Lord, was typical of the resurrection of Christ. Paul says, in speaking of the resurrection of the Lord and of all His people: '*Christ the first fruits; afterward they that are Christ's at His coming.*' 1 Corinthians 15:23. Like the wave sheaf, which was the first ripe grain gathered *before* the harvest, Christ is the first fruits of that immortal harvest of redeemed ones that at the future resurrection *shall* be gathered into the garner of God. ... In like manner the *types which relate to the second advent must be fulfilled at the time pointed out in the symbolic service*" (GC 399.2, 4).

Has this been fulfilled, yet? No! None of these things have happened, yet. Christ instituted a feast to *replace* the Jewish Passover. Why, if all the others were done away with? Nowhere in Scripture does it state that any of the other festivals or feasts were done away with or replaced. Only the evil one would want us not to study *what the feasts represent*.

In Matthew, chapter 5, Jesus said: "For verily I say unto you, Till heaven and earth pass, one jot or one tittle shall in no wise pass from the law, till all be fulfilled. Whosoever therefore shall break one of these least commandments, and shall teach men so, he shall be called the least in the kingdom of heaven: but whosoever shall do and teach them, the same shall be called great in the kingdom of heaven" (Matt. 5:18, 19).

"And he said unto them, With desire I have desired to eat this passover with you before I suffer: for I say unto you, I will not any more eat thereof, until it be *fulfilled in the kingdom of God*" (Luke 22:15, 16).

The Sabbath and Other Feasts

"Again the people were *reminded of the sacred obligation of the Sabbath*. Yearly feasts were appointed, at which all the men of the nation were to assemble before the Lord, bringing to Him their offerings of gratitude and the first fruits of His bounties. The object of all these regulations was stated: they proceeded from no exercise of mere arbitrary sovereignty; all were given for the good of Israel. The Lord said, 'Ye shall be holy men unto Me' [Exodus 22:31]— worthy to be acknowledged by a holy God. *These laws* were to be recorded by Moses, and carefully treasured as the *foundation of the national law, and, with the ten precepts which they were given to illustrate, the condition of the fulfillment of God's promises to Israel*" (PP 311.2, 3).

Note:

1. As we seek to "restore the principles that are foundational to the kingdom of God," read again the quotation above.
2. Which statutes were given to "guard" the *Sabbath*? What was Ellen White saying is foundational? *Why is it foundational?*
3. Ellen White, in speaking of the camp meetings, referred to them as feasts.

"*Do you want to find Jesus? He is at the feast. You may find him here. He has come up to the feast. There are men and women that have brought him with them; and now we want you to press through, and touch the hem of his garment, that you may receive of the virtue that is found in him, and triumph in the God of your salvation*" (Review and Herald, Aug. 17, 1869, Art. B, par. 3).

"*In the days of Christ these feasts were attended by vast multitudes of people from all lands; and had they been kept as God intended, in the spirit of true worship, the light of truth might through them have been given to all the nations of the world*" (6T 39.4).

"If the children of Israel needed the benefit of these holy convocations in their time, how much more do we need them in these last days of peril and conflict! And if the people of the world then needed the light which God had committed to His church, how much more do they need it now!" (6T 40.2).

"The regulations observed in the encampment of the Israelites are an example to us. It was Christ who gave those special instructions to Israel, and He intended them for us also, upon whom the ends of the world are come. We should study carefully the specifications of God's word and practice these directions as the will of God" (6T 34.4).

"They were instructed by the Lord. He withheld from them nothing favorable to the formation of characters which would make them fit representatives of His kingdom. *Their feasts, the Passover, the Pentecost, and the Feast of Tabernacles, and the ceremonies attending these gatherings, were to proclaim the truths that God had entrusted to His people.* At these gatherings the people were to show gladness and joy, expressing their thanksgiving for their privileges and the gracious treatment of their Lord. Thus they were to show to a world that knew not God that the Lord does not forsake those who trust in Him. With joyful voices they were to sing, 'Why art thou cast down, O my soul? and why art thou disquieted within me? hope in God: for I shall yet praise him, who is the health of my countenance, and my God.' Ps. 43:5" (UL 232.3).

"The people of Israel, as they journeyed through the wilderness, praised God in sacred song. The commandments and promises of the Lord were set to music, and all along the journey these were sung by the pilgrim travelers. And in Canaan as they met at their sacred feasts God's wonderful works were to be recounted, and grateful thanksgiving was to be offered to His name. God desired that the whole life of His people should be a life of praise. Thus His way was to be made 'known upon earth,' His 'saving health among all nations.' Psalm 67:2.

"So it should be now. The people of the world are worshiping false gods. They are to be turned from their false worship, not by hearing denunciation of their idols, but by beholding something better. God's goodness is to be made known. 'Ye are My witnesses, saith the Lord, that I am God.' Isaiah 43:12" (COL 298.4, 299.1).

Sabbath

The first feast, *Sabbath*, is found in Leviticus, chapter 23, verses 2 to 4: "Speak unto the children of Israel, and say unto them, Concerning the feasts ["an appointed time," H4150] of the LORD, which ye shall proclaim to be holy convocations, even these are my feasts [H4150]. Six days shall work be done: but the seventh day is the sabbath of rest, an holy convocation; ye shall do no work therein: it is the sabbath of the LORD in all your dwellings. These are the feasts of the LORD, even holy convocations, which ye shall proclaim in their seasons."

- It had four sacrifices, one more than Passover, two times daily, and two special *Sabbath sacrifices in the temple*, and these are listed in Numbers. "And on the sabbath day two lambs of the first year without spot, and two tenth deals of flour for a meat offering, mingled with oil, and the drink offering thereof: this is the burnt offering of every sabbath, *beside* the continual burnt offering, and his drink offering" (Num. 28:9, 10).
  Note: Like all the rest of the feasts, the Sabbath had special sacrifices. *Yet, this never changed the obligation to keep it—even when the sacrifices ceased!*

- It is not a statute, and *it is the only one of the feasts which is not a statute*. The seventh-day Sabbath is also described as a feast by Ellen G. White as she quotes Henry Tuberville: "As the sign of the authority of the Catholic Church, papist writers cite 'the very act of changing the Sabbath into Sunday, which Protestants allow of; … because by keeping Sunday, they acknowledge the church's power to ordain *feasts*, and to command them under sin.'—Henry Tuberville, *An Abridgment of the Christian Doctrine*, page 58. What then is the change of the Sabbath, but the sign, or mark, of the authority of the Roman Church—'the mark of the beast'?" (GC 448.1).

- It is a commandment: "Remember the sabbath day, to keep it holy" (Exod. 20:8). "Six days shall work be done: but the seventh day is the sabbath of rest, an holy convocation; ye shall do no work therein: it is the Sabbath [H7676] of the LORD in all your dwellings" (Lev. 23:3).

- Like all the other feasts, it is a holy *convocation* ["a meeting," a rehearsal for heaven, H4744]. In Leviticus, God is telling us to meet on Sabbath: "Speak unto the children of Israel, and say unto them, Concerning the feasts of the LORD, which ye shall proclaim to be *holy convocations*, even these are my feasts" (Lev. 23:2).
  Note: This is the only place we have found in Old Testament Scripture where we are commanded to have convocation on the Sabbath!

- It is a *feast* [a *moed*, "an appointed time," H4150] : "Speak unto the children of Israel, and say unto them, *Concerning the feasts of the LORD*, which ye shall proclaim to be holy convocations, even these are my feasts. Six days shall work be done: but the seventh day is the Sabbath of rest, an holy convocation; ye shall do no work therein: it is the sabbath of the LORD in all your dwellings. These are the feasts of the LORD, even holy convocations, which ye shall proclaim in their seasons" (Lev. 23:2–4; see the section "What Are *Moeds*?" above).

- It is the Lord's "*Sabbath*," [H7676], one of *three* "sabbaths" designated by H7676.
- It is an *everlasting covenant* and sign between us and God: "Wherefore the children of Israel shall keep the sabbath, to observe the sabbath throughout their generations, for a *perpetual* ["everlasting," H5769] covenant. It is a sign between me and the children of Israel *for ever* ["everlasting," H5769]: for in six days the LORD made heaven and earth, and on the seventh day he rested, and was refreshed" (Exod. 31:16, 17; see the section "Isaiah and the Curses" in chapter V).

Who changed the Sabbath? Constantine did, in 321 A.D. (Philip Schaff, *History of the Christian Church*, vol. 3, p. 31). The Catholic Church, at the First Council of Niceae, in 325, changed Passover to Easter. Eusebius, *Ecclesiastical History*, vol. 24, pp. 9–11; *Seventh-day Adventist Bible Studies Source Book*, p. 362, 363. Later all the feast days were abolished. Bishop T. Enright, bishop of St. Alphonsus' Rock Church states: "The Catholic Church abolished not only the Sabbath, but all the other Jewish festivals" (Letter, St. Louis, June 1905, at http://www.iaua.name/Letter.html).

Passover

The second feast is *Passover*: "In the fourteenth day of the first month at even is the LORD's Passover" (Lev. 23:5).

- The feast had three sacrifices, one less than the seventh-day Sabbath. Two were those offered daily in the temple, and then there was the Passover lamb, which was eaten by the family.
- Jerusalem is no longer the place of the feasts. "Jesus saith unto her, Woman, believe me, the hour cometh, when ye shall *neither in this mountain, nor yet at Jerusalem*, worship the Father. Ye worship ye know not what: we know what we worship: for salvation is of the Jews. *But the hour cometh, and now is*, when the true worshippers shall worship the Father in spirit and in truth: for the Father seeketh such to worship him. God is a Spirit: and they that worship him must worship him in spirit and in truth" (John 4:21–24).

- It is an *everlasting statute:* "And this day shall be unto you for a memorial; and ye shall keep it a feast to the LORD throughout your generations; ye shall keep it a feast by an *ordinance* ["statute," H2708] *for ever* ["everlasting," H5769]. And ye shall observe the feast of unleavened bread; for in this selfsame day have I brought your armies out of the land of Egypt: therefore shall ye observe this day in your generations by an *ordinance* ["statute," H2708] *for ever* [everlasting– H5769]. And ye shall observe this thing for an *ordinance* ["statute," H2708] to thee and to thy sons *for ever* ["everlasting," H5769]" (Exod. 12:14, 17, 24).
- It is a holy *convocation* ["a meeting," a rehearsal for heaven, H4744]: "Speak unto the children of Israel, and say unto them, Concerning the feasts of the LORD, which ye shall proclaim to be holy convocations, even these are my feasts" (Lev. 23:2). It is to be held in our houses, not in the temple (see Exod. 12:3, 4, 22, 40, 46; Lev. 23:14).
- It is a *feast* ["a *moed*, an appointed time," H4150] found in Leviticus, chapter 23: "These are the feasts of the LORD, even holy convocations, which ye shall proclaim in their seasons" (Lev. 23:4).
- Passover was re-instituted per Jesus: *"Christ, having eaten the Passover with His disciples, instituted that feast which was to commemorate His own death as the Lamb of God, which taketh away the sin of the world"* (GC 399.3).
- We will keep Passover in heaven: "I will not drink henceforth of this fruit of the vine, until that day when I drink it new with you in my Father's kingdom" (Matt. 26:29).
- "The Passover was to be both commemorative and typical, not only pointing back to the deliverance from Egypt, but forward to the greater deliverance which Christ was to accomplish in freeing His people from the bondage of sin" (PP 277.1).

Unleavened Bread

The third feast is the *Feast of Unleavened Bread*. It is found in Leviticus, chapter 23, verse 6: "And on the fifteenth day of the same month is the feast of unleavened bread unto the LORD: seven days ye must eat unleavened bread."

- The feast had 28 sacrifices, two daily, plus one special offering consisting of several animals and an additional sin offering on each of the seven days of Unleavened Bread. These are listed in Numbers 28:17–31 and Leviticus 23:8.

- It is an *everlasting statute:* "And ye shall eat neither bread, nor parched corn, nor green ears, until the selfsame day that ye have brought an offering unto your God: it shall be a statute *for ever* ["everlasting," H5769] throughout your generations *in all your dwellings*" (Lev. 23:14).
- It is a holy *convocation* ["a meeting," a rehearsal for heaven, H4744]: "Speak unto the children of Israel, and say unto them, Concerning the feasts of the LORD, which ye shall proclaim to be holy convocations, even these are my feasts" (Lev. 23:2).
- It is a *feast* [a *moed,* "an appointed time," H4150] found in Leviticus, chapter 23, verse 4: "These are the feasts of the LORD, even holy convocations, which ye shall proclaim in their seasons."
- *Its final fulfillment is still pending.* Paul says in speaking of the resurrection of the Lord and of all His people: "Christ the firstfruits; afterward they that are Christ's at his coming" (1 Cor. 15:23).
- "Like the wave sheaf, which was the first ripe grain gathered before the harvest, Christ is the first fruits of that immortal harvest of redeemed ones that at the future resurrection shall be gathered into the garner of God" (GC 399.2).
- It was required of all the men of Israel: "Three times in a year shall all thy males appear before the LORD thy God in the place which he shall choose; in the feast of unleavened bread ..." (Deut. 16:16).
- Jerusalem is no longer the place of the feasts (John 4:21–24).
- In Revelation 14, the future final fulfillment of the wave offering of firstfruits is pictured in those singing a new song before the throne: "... and no man could learn that song but the hundred and forty and four thousand, which were redeemed from the earth. These were redeemed from among men, being the firstfruits unto God and to the Lamb" (Rev. 14:3, 4).

Theologians have endeavored to define a "feast of firstfruits" (which is just another name for unleavened bread) as a separate feast to avoid dealing with the Sabbath as one of the feasts. This way the feasts still total seven without including the Sabbath. However, the scriptural evidence for this interpretation is lacking. Firstfruits is mentioned with Pentecost also. In Leviticus 23, it was within the week of unleavened bread. It is not designated a *moed* [H4150]. It is not designated a "holy convocation separated by God as described in the *moeds* [H4150].

The *offering* of firstfruits symbolized Christ's resurrection (1 Cor. 15: 20, 23). The *feast days* were not offerings, but contained offerings, as did the Sabbath.

Pentecost—Feast of Weeks

The fourth feast is the *Feast of Weeks*. It is found in Leviticus, chapter 23, verses 15 and 16: "And ye shall count unto you from the morrow after the sabbath, from the day that ye brought the sheaf of the wave offering; seven sabbaths shall be complete: even unto the morrow after the seventh sabbath shall ye number fifty days; and ye shall offer a new meat offering unto the LORD."

- The feast had one special offering consisting of *several* animals, two daily sacrifices, plus one sin offering and two lambs for a peace offering for a total of five sacrifices. These are listed in Numbers 28:3, 4, 27–31; Leviticus 23:18, 19.
- It is an *everlasting statute*: "And ye shall proclaim on the selfsame day, that it may be an holy convocation unto you: ye shall do no servile work therein: it shall be a statute for ever ["everlasting," H5769] in all your dwellings throughout your generations" (Lev. 23:21).
- It is a holy *convocation* ["a meeting," a rehearsal for heaven, H4744]: "Speak unto the children of Israel, and say unto them, Concerning the feasts of the LORD, which ye shall proclaim to be holy convocations, even these are my feasts" (Lev. 23:2).
- It is a *feast* ["a *moed*, an appointed time," H4150] found in Leviticus, chapter 23: "These are the *feasts* of the LORD, even holy *convocations*, which ye shall proclaim in their seasons" (Lev. 23:4).
  Note: *Its final fulfillment is still pending.* "In like manner the *types which relate to the second advent must be fulfilled at the time pointed out in the symbolic service*" (GC 399.4). It is to be held in our dwellings, not in the temple (see Lev. 23:21).

The Final Fulfillment

"In immediate connection with the scenes of the great day of God, the Lord by the prophet Joel has promised a special manifestation of His Spirit. Joel 2:28. *This prophecy received a partial fulfillment in the outpouring of the Spirit on the Day of Pentecost; but it will reach its full accomplishment in the manifestation of divine grace which will attend the closing work of the gospel*" (Introduction, GC ix.3).

"And it shall come to pass afterward, that I will pour out my spirit upon all flesh; and your sons and your daughters shall prophesy, your old men shall dream dreams, your young men shall see visions" (Joel 2:28).

- It was required of all the men of Israel: "Three times in a year shall all thy males appear before the LORD thy God in the place which *he shall choose*; … in the feast of weeks …" (Deut. 16:16).
- Jerusalem is no longer the place of the feasts (John 4:21–24).
- It is to be held in our dwellings, not the temple (see Lev. 23:21).

Trumpets

The fifth feast is the *Feast of Trumpets*: "Speak unto the children of Israel, saying, In the seventh month, in the first day of the month, shall ye have a sabbath, a *memorial of blowing of trumpets*, an holy convocation" (Lev. 23:24).

- The feast had five sacrifices, two times daily, and one specialty offering of several animals, as well as the monthly sacrifices which occurred on the first of every month, plus a kid of the goats for a sin offering (see Num. 28:3, 4, 11; Num. 29:2–5).
- It is a *statute*, but not an everlasting statute: "Blow up the trumpet in the new moon, in the time appointed, on our solemn feast day. For this was a statute for Israel, and a law of the God of Jacob. This he ordained in Joseph for a testimony, when he went out through the land of Egypt: where I heard a language that I understood not" (Ps. 81:3–5). **Note:** Like the Sabbath, this statute was kept prior to the giving of the law, commandments, statutes, and judgments on Mount Sinai (see Ps. 81:3–5).
- It is a sabbath and a holy convocation: "Speak unto the children of Israel, saying, In the seventh month, in the first day of the month, shall ye have a *sabbath* [H7677], a memorial of blowing of trumpets, *an holy convocation* ["a meeting," a rehearsal for heaven, H4744]" (Lev. 23:24).
- It is a feast [a *moed*, "an appointed time," H4150]: "These are the feasts of the LORD, even holy convocations, which ye shall proclaim in their seasons" (Lev. 23:4).

- Jerusalem is no longer the place of the feasts (see John 4:21–24).
  Note: *This feast has never had one fulfillment yet!* Its final fulfilment is still pending.

Atonement

The sixth feast is the *Day of Atonement*. It is found in Leviticus 23, verse 27: "Also on the tenth day of this seventh month there shall be a day of atonement: it shall be an holy convocation unto you; and ye shall afflict your souls, and offer an offering made by fire unto the LORD."

- It had five sacrifices, two times daily, and three on the Day of Atonement (Lev. 16:3–11, 23, 24; Num. 28:9–11). This was one more than on the Sabbath of the Lord.
- It is an everlasting statute: "It shall be a sabbath of rest unto you, and ye shall afflict your souls, by a statute *for ever* ["everlasting," H5769]. It shall be unto you a sabbath of rest, and ye shall afflict your souls: in the ninth day of the month at even, from even unto even, shall ye celebrate your sabbath" (Lev. 23:31, 32).
- It is a holy *convocation* ["a meeting," a rehearsal for heaven, H4744]: "These are the feasts of the LORD, even holy convocations, which ye shall proclaim in their seasons. Also on the tenth day of this seventh month there shall be a day of atonement: it shall be an holy convocation unto you; and ye shall afflict your souls, and offer an offering made by fire unto the LORD" (Lev. 23:4, 27).
- It is a *feast* ["a *moed*, an appointed time," H4150] found in Leviticus, chapter 23: "Speak unto the children of Israel, and say unto them, Concerning the feasts of the LORD, which ye shall proclaim to be holy convocations, even these are my feasts. These are the feasts of the LORD, even holy convocations, which ye shall proclaim in their seasons" (Lev. 23:2, 4).
- It is our Sabbath (lit. "your *sabbath*") [H7676]. The same word *shabbat* is used for the Lord's sabbath. "It shall be unto you a sabbath [H7676] of rest, and ye shall afflict your souls: in the ninth day of the month at even, from even unto even, shall ye celebrate *your sabbath* [H7676]" (Lev. 23:32).
- It is celebrated in "all your dwellings," not in the temple (see Lev. 23:31, 32).
- The atonement is not ended:

Aaron "came forth from that work to bless the congregation, as Christ will come forth to bless His waiting people when His work of atonement in their behalf shall be ended" (PP 426.1).
Note: Why is the Day of Atonement *our* sabbath? What does it reveal of God's plan of salvation and the future judgment?

- It is accompanied by the affliction of our souls, fasting from the evening of the ninth day to the evening of the tenth day. Adventists believe it is occurring now anti- typically. It will end at the Second Coming.
- Jerusalem is no longer the place of the feasts (John 4:21–24).

Tabernacles

The seventh feast is the *Feast of Tabernacles*: "Speak unto the children of Israel, saying, The fifteenth day of this seventh month shall be the feast of tabernacles for seven days unto the LORD" (Lev. 23:34).

- The feast had multiple sacrifices—one specialty offering, consisting of several animals each day, plus one sin offering, plus the two daily sacrifices, for a total of thirty-two sacrifices over the eight days: "Seven days ye shall offer an offering made by fire unto the LORD: on the eighth day shall be an holy convocation unto you; and ye shall offer an offering made by fire unto the LORD: it is a solemn assembly; and ye shall do no servile work therein" (Num. 29:12–38).
- It is an everlasting statute: "And ye shall keep it a feast unto the LORD seven days in the year. It shall be a statute *for ever* ["everlasting," H5769] in your generations: ye shall celebrate it in the seventh month" (Lev. 23:41).
- It has two holy *convocations* ["a meeting," a rehearsal for heaven, H4744]: "On the first day shall be an holy *convocation*: ye shall do no servile work therein. Seven days ye shall offer an offering made by fire unto the LORD: on the eighth day shall be an holy *convocation* unto you; and ye shall offer an offering made by fire unto the LORD: it is a solemn assembly [H6116]; and ye shall do no servile work therein" (Lev. 23:35, 36).
- Tabernacles is celebrated in booths, not in the temple (see Lev. 23:40, 41).
- Its fulfilment is still pending. "In the parable, when the bridegroom came, 'they that were ready went in with him to the marriage.' The coming of the bridegroom, here brought to view, takes place before

the marriage. The marriage represents the reception by Christ of His kingdom. ... In the Revelation the people of God are said to be the guests at the marriage supper. Revelation 19:9. ... Having received the kingdom, He will come in His glory, as King of kings and Lord of lords, for the redemption of His people, who are to 'sit down with Abraham, and Isaac, and Jacob," at His table in His kingdom (Matthew 8:11; Luke 22:30), to partake of the marriage supper of the Lamb" (GC 426.2).

- It has two *sabbaths* [H7677]; the first and eighth days: "Also in the fifteenth day of the seventh month, when ye have gathered in the fruit of the land, ye shall keep a feast unto the LORD seven days: on the first day shall be a sabbath, and on the eighth day shall be a sabbath" (Lev. 23:39).
- It is a feast [a *moed*, "an appointed time," H4150] found in Leviticus, chapter 23: "These are the feasts of the LORD, even holy convocations, which ye shall proclaim in their seasons" (Lev. 23:4).
- It was required of all the men of Israel: "Three times in a year shall all thy males appear before the LORD thy God in the place which he shall choose; in the feast of unleavened bread, and in the feast of weeks, and in the feast of tabernacles" (Deut. 16:16).
- Jerusalem is no longer the place of the feasts (see John 4:21–24).
Note: Its final fulfillment is still pending.

"The Feast of Tabernacles was not only *commemorative* but *typical*. It not only pointed back to the wilderness sojourn, but, as the feast of harvest, it celebrated the ingathering of the fruits of the earth, and pointed forward to the great day of final ingathering, when the Lord of the harvest shall send forth His reapers to gather the tares together in bundles for the fire, and to gather the wheat into His garner. At that time the wicked will all be destroyed. They will become 'as though they had not been.' Obadiah 16" (PP 541.2).

Note: Its final fulfilment is still pending. It is the feast to which Jesus alludes to in His parables in the New Testament, where people are invited but refuse to come (see Hosea 12:8, 9; Zech. 14:16–19).

CHAPTER 12

THE SABBATH OF THE SEVENTH YEAR AND THE JUBILEE

"As God spoke the day and the hour of Jesus' coming, and delivered the everlasting covenant to His people, He spoke one sentence, and then paused, while the words were rolling through the earth. The Israel of God stood with their eyes fixed upward, listening to the words as they came from the mouth of Jehovah and rolled through the earth like peals of loudest thunder. It was awfully solemn. At the end of every sentence the saints shouted, 'Glory! Hallelujah!' Their countenances were lighted up with the glory of God, and they shone with glory as did the face of Moses when he came down from Sinai. The wicked could not look upon them for the glory. And when the never-ending blessing was pronounced on those who had honored God in keeping His Sabbath holy, there was a mighty shout of victory over the beast and over his image.— Then commenced the Jubilee, when the land should rest" (EW 285, 286; LDE 272.3)

"And the LORD spake unto Moses in mount Sinai, saying, Speak unto the children of Israel, and say unto them, When ye come into the land which I give you, then shall the land keep a sabbath [H7676] unto the LORD. Six years thou shalt sow thy field, and six years thou shalt prune thy vineyard, and gather in the fruit thereof; but in the seventh year shall be a sabbath [H7676] of rest unto the land, a sabbath [H7676] for the LORD: thou shalt neither sow thy field, nor prune thy vineyard.

And thou shalt number seven sabbaths [H7676] of years unto thee, seven times seven years; and the space of the seven sabbaths [H7676] of years shall be unto thee forty and nine years. Then shalt thou cause the trumpet of the Jubilee to sound on the tenth day of the seventh month, in the day of atonement shall ye make the trumpet sound throughout all your land. And ye shall hallow the fiftieth year, and proclaim liberty throughout all the land unto all the inhabitants thereof: it shall be a Jubilee unto you; and ye shall return every man unto his possession, and ye shall return every man unto his family. A Jubilee shall that fiftieth year be unto you: ye shall not sow, neither reap that which groweth of itself in it, nor gather the grapes in it of thy vine undressed. Wherefore ye shall do my statutes, and keep my judgments, and do them; and ye shall dwell in the land in safety" (Lev. 25:1–4, 8–11, 18).

There are three sabbaths designated by H7676:

1. The *Lord's Sabbath* (the seventh day): "Six days shall work be done: but the seventh day is the sabbath of rest, an holy convocation; ye shall do no work therein: it is the sabbath of the LORD in all your dwellings" (Lev. 23:3).
2. *Man's Sabbath* (the Day of Atonement): "Ye shall do no manner of work: it shall be a statute for ever throughout your generations in all your dwellings. It shall be unto you a sabbath of rest, and ye shall afflict your souls: in the ninth day of the month at even, from even unto even, shall ye celebrate your sabbath" (Lev. 23:31, 32).
3. The *land's sabbath* (the sabbath of the seventh year): "Speak unto the children of Israel, and say unto them, When ye come into the land which I give you, then shall the land keep a sabbath unto the LORD. Six years thou shalt sow thy field, and six years thou shalt prune thy vineyard, and gather in the fruit thereof; but in the seventh year shall be a sabbath of rest unto the land, a sabbath for the LORD: thou shalt neither sow thy field, nor prune thy vineyard" (Lev. 25:2–4).

The Jubilee is also to be hallowed [H6942]: "And ye shall hallow [H6942] the fiftieth year, and proclaim liberty throughout all the land unto all the inhabitants thereof: it shall be a Jubilee unto you; and ye shall return every man unto his possession, and ye shall return every man unto his family" (Lev. 25:10). "And God blessed the seventh day, and sanctified [H6942] it: because that in it he had rested from all his work which God created and made" (Gen. 2:3). "Remember the sabbath day, to keep it holy [H6942]" (Exod. 20:8). Just like the Sabbath is sanctified ["hallowed," H6942], the Jubilee, or fiftieth year, is also hallowed, or sanctified [H6942].

As far as we know, the Jubilee has never been observed in all of Scripture (see 2 Chron. 36:21; Jer. 34:8–22). However, we know when one occurred, and by that we know when the next will occur. Christ's crucifixion occurred in AD 31 to mark that year's Jubilee. In that year, Peter proclaimed release to the captives on the day of Pentecost. He healed the lame man at the temple and then spoke of Jesus, "Whom the heaven must receive until the times of restitution of *all things*, which God hath spoken by the mouth of all his holy prophets since the world began. For Moses truly said unto the fathers, A prophet shall the Lord your God raise up unto you of your brethren, like unto me; him shall ye hear in all things whatsoever he shall say unto you" (Acts 3:21, 22).

> "As far as we know, the Jubilee has never been observed in all of Scripture."

"On the day of Pentecost Christ gave His disciples the Holy Spirit as their Comforter. It was ever to abide with His church. During the whole Jewish economy the influence of this Spirit had often been revealed in a marked manner, but not in full. The Spirit had been waiting for the crucifixion, resurrection, and ascension of Christ. For ages prayers had been offered for the fulfillment of the promise, for the impartation of the Spirit; and not one of these earnest supplications had been forgotten. Now for ten days the disciples sent up their petitions, and Christ in heaven added His intercession. He claimed the gift of the Spirit, that He might pour it out upon His people.... [Christ] having reached His throne, the Spirit was given as He had promised, and like a rushing, mighty wind, it fell upon those assembled, filling the whole house.—*Manuscript* 44, 1898" (*Christ Triumphant*, p. 301.5).

"Wherefore he saith, When he ascended up on high, he led captivity captive, and gave gifts unto men" (Eph. 4:8).

"Christ determined to bestow a gift on those who had been with Him and on those who should believe on Him, because this was the occasion of His ascension and inauguration, *a Jubilee* in heaven. What gift could Christ bestow rich enough to signalize and grace His ascension to the mediatorial throne? It must be worthy of His greatness and His royalty. Christ gave His representative, the third person of the Godhead, the Holy Spirit. This Gift could not be excelled...." (*Christ Triumphant*, p. 301.4).

"The Spirit was given as Christ had promised, and like a mighty rushing wind it fell upon those assembled, filling the whole house. It came with a fulness and power, as if for ages it had been restrained, but was now being poured forth upon the church, to be communicated to the world. What followed this outpouring?— Thousands were converted in a day. In Christ's day many heard the gospel, but they did not become sufficiently interested to search for the pearl of great price. But on the day of Pentecost three thousand were converted by the preaching of the gospel. A wonderful communication was made that day between heaven and earth. On the day of Pentecost, Christ's witnesses proclaimed the truth, telling men the wonderful news of salvation through Christ. And as a flaming two-edged sword the truth flashed conviction into human hearts. Men were brought under Christ's control. The glad tidings were carried to the uttermost bounds of the inhabited world. The church beheld converts flocking to her from all directions. The altar of the cross, which sanctifies the gift, was rebuilt. Believers were reconverted. Sinners united with Christians in seeking the pearl of great price. The prophecy was fulfilled, the weak 'shall be as David,' and David 'as the angel of the Lord.' Every Christian saw in his brother the divine similitude of benevolence and love. One interest prevailed. One object swallowed up all others. Every pulse beat in healthy concert. *The only ambition of the believers was to see who could reveal most perfectly the likeness of Christ's character, who could do the most for the enlargement of his kingdom.* 'The multitude of them that believed were of one heart and one soul.' The Spirit of Christ animated the whole congregation; for they had found the pearl of great price" (*The Watchman*, Nov. 28, 1905, par. 5–7, 9).

"As Christ arose, He brought from the grave *a multitude of captives*. The earthquake at His death had rent open their graves, and when He arose, they came forth with Him. They were those who had been co-laborers with God, and who at the cost of their lives had borne testimony to the truth. Now they were to be witnesses for Him who had raised them from the dead" (DA 786.1).

"And after Christ came up from the Resurrection, what did He do? He grasped His power and held His scepter. He opened the graves and brought up the multitude of captives, testifying to everyone in our world and in creation that He had the power over death and that He rescued the captives of death" (*Faith and Works*, p. 74.1).

"When Christ cried out while upon the cross, 'It is finished' [John 19:30], there was a mighty earthquake, that rent open the graves of many who had been faithful and loyal, bearing their testimony against every evil work, and magnifying the Lord of hosts. As the Life-giver came forth from the sepulcher, proclaiming, 'I am the resurrection, and the life' [John 11:25], He summoned these saints from the grave. When alive, they had borne their testimony unflinchingly for the truth; now, they were to be witnesses to Him who had raised them from the dead. These, said Christ, are *no longer the captives of Satan*. I have redeemed them; I have brought them from the grave as the *first fruits* of My power, to be with Me where I am, nevermore to see death or experience sorrow. During His ministry, Jesus raised the dead to life. He raised the son of the widow of Nain, the daughter of Jairus, and Lazarus; but these were not clothed with immortality. After they were raised, they continued to be subject to death. But those who came forth from the grave at Christ's resurrection were raised to everlasting life. *They were the multitude of captives that ascended with Him as trophies of His victory over death and the grave*" (1SM 304.1, 2).

"Then the high priest rose up, and all they that were with him, (which is the sect of the Sadducees,) and were filled with indignation, and laid their hands on the apostles, and put them in the common prison. But the angel of the Lord by night opened the prison doors, and brought them forth, and said, Go, stand and speak in the temple to the people all the words of this life" (Acts 5:17–20).

"Then Peter and the other apostles answered and said, We ought to obey God rather than men. The God of our fathers raised up Jesus, whom ye slew and hanged on a tree. Him hath God exalted with his right hand to be a Prince and a Saviour, for to give repentance to Israel, and forgiveness of sins. And we are his witnesses of these things; and so is also the Holy Ghost, whom God hath given to them *that obey him*" (Acts 5:29–32).

"The disciples prayed with intense earnestness for a fitness to meet men and in their daily intercourse to speak words that would lead sinners to Christ. Putting away all differences, all desire for the supremacy, they came close together in Christian fellowship. They drew nearer and nearer to God, and as they did this they realized what a privilege had been theirs in being permitted to associate so closely with Christ. Sadness filled their hearts as they thought of how many times they had grieved Him by their slowness of comprehension, their failure to understand the lessons that, for their good, He was trying to teach them" (AA 37.1).

"Thou hast ascended on high, *thou hast led captivity captive*: thou hast received gifts for men; yea, for the rebellious also, that the LORD God might dwell among them" (Ps. 68:18).

Is there a biblical precedent of punishment for not keeping the other sabbaths and the Jubilee?

"This is the word that came unto Jeremiah from the LORD, after that the king Zedekiah had made a covenant with all the people which were at Jerusalem, to proclaim liberty unto them; that every man should let his manservant, and every man his maidservant, being an Hebrew or an

Hebrewess, go free; that none should serve himself of them, to wit, of a Jew his brother. Now when all the princes, and all the people, which had entered into the covenant, heard that every one should let his manservant, and every one his maidservant, go free, that none should serve themselves of them any more, then they obeyed, and let them go. But afterward they turned, and caused the servants and the handmaids, whom they had let go free, to return, and brought them into subjection for servants and for handmaids. Therefore the word of the LORD came to Jeremiah from the LORD, saying, *Thus saith the LORD, the God of Israel; I made a covenant with your fathers in the day that I brought them forth out of the land of Egypt, out of the house of bondmen, saying, At the end of seven years let ye go every man his brother an Hebrew, which hath been sold unto thee; and when he hath served thee six years, thou shalt let him go free from thee: but your fathers hearkened not unto me, neither inclined their ear. And ye were now turned, and had done right in my sight, in proclaiming liberty every man to his neighbour; and ye had made a covenant before me in the house which is called by my name: but ye turned and polluted my name, and caused every man his servant, and every man his handmaid, whom he had set at liberty at their pleasure, to return, and brought them into subjection, to be unto you for servants and for handmaids. Therefore thus saith the LORD; ye have not hearkened unto me, in proclaiming liberty, every one to his brother, and every man to his neighbour: behold, I proclaim a liberty for you, saith the LORD, to the sword, to the pestilence, and to the famine; and I will make you to be removed into all the kingdoms of the earth.* And I will give the men that have transgressed my covenant, which have not performed the words of the covenant which they had made before me, when they cut the calf in twain, and passed between the parts thereof, The princes of Judah, and the princes of Jerusalem, the eunuchs, and the priests, and all the people of the land, which passed between the parts of the calf; I will even give them into the hand of their enemies, and into the hand of them that seek their life: and their dead bodies shall be for meat unto the fowls of the heaven, and to the beasts of the earth. And Zedekiah king of Judah and his princes will I give into the hand of their enemies, and into the hand of them that seek their life, and into the hand of the king of Babylon's army, which are gone up from you. Behold, I will command, saith the LORD, and cause them to return to this city; and they shall fight against it, and take it, and burn it with fire: and I will make the cities of Judah a desolation without an inhabitant" (Jer. 34:8–22).

This would be done to "fulfil the word of the LORD by the mouth of Jeremiah, *until the land had enjoyed her sabbaths*: for as long as she lay desolate she kept *sabbath*, to fulfil threescore and ten years" (2 Chron. 36:21).

The keeping of this sabbath is depictured as follows:

"Is not this the fast that I have chosen? to loose the bands of wickedness, to undo the heavy burdens, and to let the oppressed go free, and that ye break every yoke? Is it not to deal thy bread to the hungry, and that thou bring the poor that are cast out to thy house? when thou seest the naked, that thou cover him; and that thou hide not thyself from thine own flesh? Then shall thy light break forth as the morning, and thine health shall spring forth speedily: and thy righteousness shall go before thee; the glory of the LORD shall be thy reward. And the LORD shall guide thee continually, and satisfy thy soul in drought, and make fat thy bones: and thou shalt be like a watered garden, and like a spring of water, whose waters fail not. And they that shall be of thee shall build the old waste places: thou shalt raise up the foundations of many generations; and thou shalt be called, The repairer of the breach, the restorer of paths to dwell in" (Isa. 58:6–8, 11, 12).

"In words of unmistakable meaning the prophet points out the specific work of this remnant people who build the wall. 'If thou turn away thy foot from the Sabbath, from doing thy pleasure on My holy day; and call the Sabbath a delight, the holy of the Lord, honorable; and shalt honor Him, not doing thine own ways, nor finding thine own pleasure, nor speaking thine own words: then shalt thou delight thyself in the Lord; and I will cause thee to ride upon the high places of the earth, and feed thee with the heritage of Jacob thy father: for the mouth of the Lord hath spoken it.' Isaiah 58:13, 14" (PK 678.1).

"In the time of the end *every* divine institution is to be restored. The breach made in the law at the time the Sabbath was changed by man, is to be repaired. God's remnant people, standing before the world as reformers, are to show that the law of God is the foundation of all enduring reform and that the Sabbath of the fourth commandment is to stand as a memorial of creation, a constant reminder of the power of God. In clear, distinct lines they are to present the necessity of obedience to all the precepts of the Decalogue. Constrained by the love of Christ, they are to co-operate with Him in building up the waste places. They are to be repairers of the breach, restorers of paths to dwell in" (PK 678.2; see verse 12).

"And ye shall *hallow the fiftieth year*, and proclaim liberty throughout all the land unto all the inhabitants thereof: it shall be a jubilee unto you; and ye shall return every man unto his possession, and ye shall return every man unto his family. *A jubilee shall that fiftieth year be unto you*: ye shall not sow, neither reap that which groweth of itself in it, nor gather the grapes in it of thy vine undressed. Wherefore ye shall do my statutes, and keep my judgments, and do them; and ye shall dwell in the land in safety. And the land shall yield her fruit, and ye shall eat your fill, and dwell therein in safety. And if ye shall say, What shall we eat the seventh year? behold, we shall not sow, nor gather in our increase: then I will command my blessing upon you in the sixth year, and it shall bring forth fruit for three years. And ye shall sow the eighth year, and eat yet of old fruit until the ninth year; until her fruits come in ye shall eat of the old store" (Lev. 25:10, 11, 18–22).

Regarding the sign of the Jubilee, Isaiah wrote: "And this shall be a sign unto thee, Ye shall eat this year such as groweth of itself; and the second year that which springeth of the same: and in the third year sow ye, and reap, and plant vineyards, and eat the fruit thereof" (Isa. 37:30; also 2 Kings 19:29).

"*The Lord is coming—let this be*

The herald note of jubilee" (*Review and Herald*, Nov. 29, 1881, par. 15, from *Gems of Song*, 1870, no. 9).

"Great truths that have lain unheeded and unseen since the day of Pentecost, are to shine from God's word in their native purity" (*The Ellen G. White 1888 Materials*, p. 1651.8).

CHAPTER 13

SABBATH IN THE MIDDLE

In Leviticus, chapter 23, the Sabbath is given by God as the first of all the feasts: "Concerning the *feasts* ["appointed times," H4150] of the LORD, which ye shall proclaim to be holy *convocations* ["meetings," rehearsals for heaven, H4744], even these are my *feasts* ["appointed times," H4150]. Six days shall work be done: but the seventh day is the sabbath of rest, an holy *convocation* ["a meeting," a rehearsal for heaven, H4744]; ye shall do no work therein: it is the sabbath of the LORD in all your dwellings. These are the *feasts* ["appointed times," H4150] of the LORD, even holy *convocations* ["meetings," rehearsals for heaven, H4744], which ye shall *proclaim* [H7121] in their *seasons* ["appointed times," H4150]. These are the feasts of the LORD, even holy convocations, which ye shall proclaim in their seasons. And Moses declared unto the children of Israel the feasts [H4150] of the LORD" (Lev. 23:2–4, 44).

The Sabbath is defined as a feast day and is bracketed by these definitions two times before and two times afterward, being inextricably tied to the feast days and sacrifices. In reference to the little horn, Daniel states: "And he shall speak great words against the most High, and shall wear out the saints of the most High, and think to change times [Chaldean, "seasons," H2166] and *laws*: and they shall be given into his hand until a time [Chaldean, "set time," a year in prophetic time, H5732] and times [H5732] and the dividing of time [H5732]" (Dan. 7:25).

Note: These are God's appointed times or set times.

We tend to focus only on the Sabbath as being changed and totally disregard the fact that the other appointed times, God's feasts, were changed or eliminated, as well. We may dismiss the latter because we consider the feasts to be part of the "ceremonial law," which was nailed to the cross, so therefore we have no issue with Rome doing away with them. This could not be further from the truth!

Note: None of the days were abolished, *only* the sacrifices and ordinances associated with them.

"I will gather them that are sorrowful ["grieved, afflicted," H3013] for the *solemn assembly* ["appointed times," H4150], who are of thee, to whom the *reproach* ["disgrace," H2718] of it was a *burden*. Behold, *at that time* I will undo all that afflict thee: and I will save her that halteth, and gather her that was driven out; and I will get them praise and fame in every land where they have been put to shame" (Zeph. 3:18, 19).

Note: The text above applies to the Sabbath and the rest of the *feasts* [H4150], *not just the eighth day of Tabernacles* ["solemn assembly," H6116]. *The Sabbath is inextricably tied to the other feasts (moeds) and the sacrifices of the temple.* Compare with Leviticus 23:36.

There is no way to separate the Sabbath from the rest of the feasts or the sacrifices. Sabbath is bracketed by God's defining of the feasts with their sacrifices. It is found in the middle of the descriptions of the following texts.

Daily Sacrifices

"And the LORD spake unto Moses, saying, Command the children of Israel, and say unto them, My offering, and my bread for my sacrifices made by fire, for a sweet savour unto me, shall ye observe to offer unto me in their due season. And thou shalt say unto them, This is the offering made by fire which ye shall offer unto the LORD; two lambs of the first year without spot day by day, for a continual burnt offering. The one lamb shalt thou offer in the morning, and the other lamb shalt thou offer at even" (Num. 28:1–4).

Sabbath Sacrifices

As with the other feasts, Sabbath had *special sacrifices*.

"And on the *sabbath day* two lambs of the first year without spot, and two tenth deals of flour for a meat offering, mingled with oil, and the drink offering thereof: this is the burnt offering of every sabbath, *beside* the continual burnt offering, and his drink offering" (Num. 28:9, 10).

"These things ye shall do unto the LORD in your set feasts, beside your vows, and your freewill offerings, for your burnt offerings, and for your meat offerings, and for your drink offerings, and for your peace offerings" (Num. 29:39).

Note: The sacrifices, which occurred in the temple, were not the appointed times. Neither were they the Sabbath of the Lord, the Day of Atonement [our Sabbath], or any of the other appointed times.

The Temple

Its Sacrifices and Ceremonies

The sanctuary service is the blueprint for the plan of salvation. It is beautiful in its simplicity! It shows, in symbolic demonstrations, how God's Son planned to die for our sins and pay for them Himself. This entire service was fulfilled by Christ's sacrifice.

"And to offer all burnt sacrifices unto the LORD in the *sabbaths* [H7676, "on the seventh-day Sabbath and on the Day of Atonement," see Leviticus 23], in the *new moons*, and on the *set feasts*, by number, according to the order commanded unto them, continually before the LORD: and that they should keep the charge of the tabernacle of the congregation, and the charge of the holy place, and the charge of the sons of Aaron their brethren, in the service of the house of the LORD" (1 Chron. 23:31, 32).

"Behold, I build an house to the name of the LORD my God, to dedicate it to him, and to burn before him sweet incense, and for the continual shewbread, and for the *burnt offerings* morning and evening, *on the sabbaths* [H7676], and on the *new moons*, and on the *solemn feasts* of the LORD our God. This is an ordinance for ever to Israel" (2 Chron. 2:4).

"Then Solomon offered burnt offerings unto the LORD on the altar of the LORD, which he had built before the porch, even after a certain rate every day, offering according to the commandment of Moses, on the *sabbaths* [H7676], and on the *new moons*, and on the *solemn feasts*, three times in the year, even in the *feast of unleavened bread*, and in the *feast of weeks*, and in the *feast of tabernacles*" (2 Chron. 8:12, 13).

Note: The use of "sabbaths," in the plural form in Hebrew scripture, applies to the Lord's Sabbath, our Sabbath and the land's Sabbath. All of these had the same Hebrew word to denote them [*shabbath*, H7676], in contrast to the other little sabbaths [H7677].

"He appointed also the king's portion of his substance for the burnt offerings, to wit, for the morning and evening burnt offerings, and the burnt offerings for the *sabbaths* [H7676], and for the *new moons*, and for the *set feasts*, as it is written in the law of the LORD" (2 Chron. 31:3).

"For the shewbread, and for the continual meat offering, and for the continual burnt offering, of the *sabbaths*, of the *new moons*, for the *set feasts*, and for the holy things, and for the sin offerings to make an atonement for Israel, and for all the work of the house of our God" (Neh. 10:33).

Note: The Sabbath, the feasts, the temple, the sacrifices and the priesthood were bound together by God. If we throw away the feasts because of the sacrifices which *prefigured Christ's sacrifice*, we make our own *anti-Sabbath law*. The temple service, the sacrifices, the priesthood and the offerings all prefigured Christ, and, in Daniel, it is prophesied that these good things would be fulfilled in Christ. *The Sabbath is tied to the feasts*. If we throw away the feasts because they are associated with the temple, the priesthood, and the sacrifices, we discard the Sabbath as a tenable doctrine of the church!

> "If we throw away the feasts because of the sacrifices which prefigured Christ's sacrifice, we make our own anti-Sabbath law."

Note: The sacrificial system, showing the price paid by God for our sins, was fulfilled in Christ's sacrifice on the cross. *The moeds, including the Sabbath of the Lord, which show the path from sin to righteousness remain and will always remain!*

CHAPTER 14

THE EARLY CHURCH AND THE FEASTS

In the early church, the western church—the church of Rome—persecuted the eastern churches regarding when to celebrate the resurrection of the Lord. The persecution culminated in 325 A.D. at the Council of Nicea. "In 325 the Council of Nicaea *decreed* that Easter should be observed on the first Sunday following the first full moon after the spring equinox (March 21). Easter, therefore, can fall on any Sunday between March 22 and April 25" (Hans J. Hillerbrand, "Easter holiday (Pascha)," at https://britannica.com/topic/Easter-holiday). This is in contrast to the scriptural reckoning of this date.

Paul was keeping the feasts in A.D. 57 (see the section "Paul" in chapter VI of this book.) Eusebius quotes Polycrates from the second century:

"All of these kept the fourteenth day of the month as the beginning of the Paschal festival, in accordance with the Gospel, not deviating in the least but following the rule of the faith. Last of all I too, Polycrates, the least of you all, act according to the tradition of my family, some members of which I have actually followed; for seven of them were bishops and I am the eighth, and my family have always kept the day when the people put away the leaven. So I, my friends, after spending *sixty-five years* in the Lord's service and conversing with Christians from all parts of the world, and going carefully through all Holy Scripture, am not scared of threats. Better people than I have said: 'We must obey God rather than men.' [Acts 5:29]" (*The Seventh-day Adventist Bible Commentary*, vol. 9, p. 362).

CHAPTER 15

THE SIGNIFICANCE OF THE FEAST DAYS

God declares that these three feasts are required of all the men of Israel. Why?

1. Unleavened Bread—our acceptance of Christ's sacrifice and life
2. Pentecost—our acceptance of the law and the gift of the Holy Spirit to keep it and the sanctification God provides
3. Tabernacles—our life with God—dwelling in His presence, the marriage feast.

Salvation in 3-D

The feasts are about what God has done and will do for us. They are God's plan of salvation shown in 3-D. They help us know who God is, how much He loves us, and where He wants to lead us. They are a recognition of God's power over time and space and His sovereignty in our lives! They are commemorative and prophetic.

Did Jesus ever tell parables about inviting people to a wedding feast, dinner, or supper?

By refusing to go to the great supper, the wedding feast, the feast to celebrate our brothers and sisters' salvation, we show our unfitness to enter heaven. By refusing the wedding garment He provides, we show that we don't know Him. Our submission to Him in *all* things shows we trust our Father's will, who *has* saved us.

The weekly Sabbath and the little sabbaths show our recognition of God's sovereignty and power over time, sin, our problems—over everything. Our observing them is our way of saying, "Thank you!"

Or, is there a problem with spending more time with God?

Rest is the cornerstone of God's kingdom; the Sabbath and feasts typify this rest. Looking at the following statement, we see how God takes seriously any infraction of His law:

"The fact that the holy pair in disregarding the prohibition of God in one particular, thus transgressed his law, and as the result suffered the consequences of the fall, should impress all with a just sense of the sacred character of the law of God. If the experience of our first parents in the transgression of what many who profess to fear God would call *the lesser requirements* of the law of God, was attended with such fearful consequences, what will be the punishment of those who not only break its most important precepts, as clearly defined as is the fourth commandment, but also teach others to transgress?" (*Review and Herald*, May 6, 1875, par. 1; see PP 311.2, 3).

> The weekly Sabbath and the little sabbaths show our recognition of God's sovereignty and power over time, sin, our problems—over everything.

What law was given to man on Mount Sinai? Was it just the Ten Commandments? Is the "Moral Law" just the Ten Commandments? Nehemiah and Ellen White answer these questions:

In *Patriarchs and Prophets*, Ellen G. White quotes Nehemiah: "Concerning the law proclaimed from Sinai, Nehemiah says, 'Thou camest down also upon mount Sinai, and spakest with them from heaven, and gavest them *right judgments, and true laws, good statutes and commandments*:' Nehemiah 9:13" (PP 365.2, emphasis supplied by Ellen G. White).

"In consequence of continual transgression, the *moral law* was *repeated* in awful grandeur *from Sinai*. Christ gave to Moses religious precepts which were to govern the everyday life. These *statutes* were explicitly given to *guard* the ten commandments. They *were not shadowy types to pass away with the death of Christ*. They *were to be binding upon man in every age as long as time should last*. These commands were enforced by the power of the moral law, and they clearly and definitely *explained* that law" (*Review and Herald*, May 6, 1875, par. 10).

In two places in Ellen G. White's writings, she quotes Romans 7:12 this way:

"For the divine *statutes*, which are 'holy and just and good' (Romans 7:12), men were endeavoring to substitute laws to suit the purpose of their own selfish and cruel hearts" (PP 123.1).

"Men had well-nigh lost the knowledge of the true God. Their minds were darkened by idolatry. For the divine *statutes*, which are 'holy, and just, and good' [Romans 7:12], men were endeavoring to substitute laws in harmony with the purposes of their own cruel, selfish hearts" (PK 15.2).

"... the great Lawgiver is requiring justice of those who have had His holy law in derision and have called it 'a curse to man,' 'miserable,' and 'rickety.' When such feel the iron grasp of this law taking hold of them, these expressions will appear before them in living characters, and they will then realize the sin of having that law in derision which the Word of God calls '*holy*, *just*, and *good*' " (EW 65.2).

Note: Ellen G. White equates the law [*nomos*, G3551] with the statutes.

"Ezra became a mouthpiece for God, educating those about him in the *principles that govern heaven*" (PK 609.2).

"*Moses* of himself *framed no law. Christ*, the angel whom God had appointed to go before his chosen people, *gave to Moses statutes and requirements* necessary to a living religion and to *govern* the people of God. Christians commit a terrible mistake in calling this law severe and arbitrary, and then contrasting it with the gospel and mission of Christ in his ministry on earth, as though he were in opposition to the *just precepts* which they call the law of Moses" (*Review and Herald*, May 6, 1875, par. 12).

In her *Review and Herald* article of May 6, 1875, Ellen G. White states: "Professed Christians now cry, Christ! Christ is our righteousness, but away with the law. They talk and act as though Christ's mission to a fallen world was for the express purpose of nullifying his Father's law. Could not that work have been just as well executed without the only beloved of the Father coming to this world and enduring grief, privation, and the shameful death of the cross? Ministers preach that the atonement gave men liberty to break the law of God, and to commit sin, and then praise the free grace and mercy revealed through Christ under the gospel, while they despise the law of God. They cast aside the restraint of the law, and give loose rein to the corrupt passions and the promptings of the natural heart, and then triumph in the mercy and grace of the gospel. Christ speaks to such: 'Not every one that saith unto me, Lord, Lord, shall enter into the kingdom of heaven; but he that doeth the will of my Father which is in heaven.' *What is the will of the Father? That we keep his commandments.* Christ, to *enforce* the will of his Father, became the *author of the statutes and precepts given through Moses* to the people of God. Christians who extol Christ, but array themselves against the law governing the Jewish church, array Christ against Christ" (*Review and Herald*, May 6, 1875, par. 15, 16).

Note: Christ is the author of the statutes and precepts of Moses.

God knew His people would have much difficulty in fulfilling their promise to serve Him with perfect obedience.

"He did not even then trust His precepts to the memory of a people who were prone to forget His requirements, but wrote them upon tables of stone. He would *remove* from Israel *all possibility of mingling heathen traditions with His holy precepts*, or of *confounding His requirements with human ordinances or customs*. But *He did not stop with giving them the precepts of the Decalogue*. The people had shown themselves so easily led astray that *He would leave no door of temptation unguarded*. Moses was commanded to write, as God should bid him, *judgments* and *laws* giving minute instruction as to what was *required*. These *directions* relating to the duty of the people to God, to one another, and to the stranger *were* only the *principles* of the Ten Commandments *amplified* and *given in* a *specific manner, that none need err*. They were *designed to guard* the *sacredness of the ten precepts* engraved on the tables of stone. And *had the people practiced the principles* of the Ten Commandments, *there would have been no need of* the *additional directions* given to Moses" (PP 364.1, 2).

Have we, as God's people, reached a point where we are practicing the principles of the Ten Commandments and no longer need further instruction in fulfilling our promise to serve Him with perfect obedience? Are we no longer required to be obedient to God? Jesus answers this question: "Be ye therefore perfect [G5046, "complete"], even as your Father which is in heaven is perfect" (Matt. 5:48). If it were not possible to keep His commandments, Jesus would not have *commanded* us to do so. Jesus' commandments are not burdensome: "For this commandment which I command you today is not too difficult for you, nor is it out of reach. By this we know that we love the children of God, when we love God, and keep his commandments. For this is the love of God, that we keep his commandments: and his commandments are not grievous" (Deut. 30:11; 1 John 5:2, 3, New American Standard Bible, 1995).

Note: The texts above show God's regard, in the Old and New Testaments, for His law. This is why God gave us grace! To make up for imperfect obedience, not to allow for rebellion.

CHAPTER 16

QUESTIONS BY AND FOR A SEVENTH-DAY ADVENTIST MINISTER

A prominent theologian in the Seventh-day Adventist Church, after reviewing an early manuscript to this book, made the following *statement*, and asked the following questions.

1. "Yes, the statutes are repeatedly mentioned."
Answer: No, the statutes are enjoined, commanded, and demanded by God.

A. They are required for sanctification (Lev. 20:8).
B. Not only are they required for sanctification but also for life (Ezek. 20:11–13, 16, 19–21, 37, 38, 47).
Notice how they are connected with the sabbaths.
Note: In *Prophets and Kings*, p. 181, Ellen G. White expanded upon the sabbaths by quoting Deuteronomy 5:12 and the above texts in Ezekiel. When the commandments are given in Exodus and Deuteronomy, why did Ellen White quote from Moses' repetition of the commandments in Deuteronomy? In Deuteronomy 5, God commands the keeping of the statutes and judgments. On page 182 of *Prophets and Kings*, she states: "In calling the attention of Judah to the sins that finally brought upon them the Babylonian Captivity, the Lord declared: 'Thou hast ... profaned My Sabbaths.' 'Therefore have I poured out Mine indignation upon them; I have consumed them with the fire

of My wrath: their own way have I recompensed upon their heads.' Ezekiel 22:8, 31" (PK 182.1).
C. God even notes our attitudes toward His statutes and connects our obedience to them through His covenant with us. "But if ye will not hearken unto me, and will not do all these commandments; and if ye shall despise my statutes, or if your soul abhor my judgments, so that ye will not do all my commandments, but that ye break my covenant" (Lev. 26:14, 15).
Note: God equates the statutes and judgments with His commandments and ultimately with the covenants He has made with us!
D. "He that rejecteth me, and receiveth not my words, hath one that judgeth him: the word that I have spoken, the same shall judge him in the last day" (John 12:48). Note what Jesus equates His words with: "For had ye believed Moses, ye would have believed me; for he wrote of me. But if ye believe not his writings, how shall ye believe my words?" (John 5:46, 47). "Whosoever therefore shall break one of these least ["least in size, amount, dignity, etc." G1646] commandments, and shall teach men so, he shall be called the least [G1646] in the kingdom of heaven: but whosoever shall do and teach them, the same shall be called great in the kingdom of heaven" (Matt. 5:19).
Note: The writings of Moses are equated with Christ's words, which will judge the world.

"It is not faith that claims the favor of Heaven without complying with the conditions upon which *mercy* is to be granted, it is presumption; for genuine faith has its foundation in the promises and provisions of the Scriptures. Let none deceive themselves with the belief that they can become holy while willfully violating one of God's *requirements*. The commission of a known sin silences the witnessing voice of the Spirit and separates the soul from God. 'Sin is the transgression of the law.' And 'whosoever sinneth [transgresseth the law] hath not seen Him, neither known Him.' 1 John 3:6. Though John in his epistles dwells so fully upon love, yet he does not hesitate to reveal the true character of that class who claim to be sanctified while living in transgression of the law of God. 'He that saith, I know Him, and keepeth not His commandments, is a liar, and the truth is not in him. But whoso keepeth His word, in him verily is the love of God perfected.' 1 John 2:4, 5. Here is the test of every man's profession. We cannot accord holiness to any man without bringing him to the measurement of God's only standard of holiness in heaven and in earth. If men feel no weight of the moral law, if they belittle and make light of God's precepts, if they break *one of the least of these commandments*, and teach men so, they shall be of no esteem in the sight of Heaven, and we may know that their claims are without foundation" (GC 472.2, 3).

Note: See how Ellen G. White defines "the law of God" in the *Review and Herald*, May 6, 1875.

Question 1: Does Ellen G. White speak unequivocally of celebrating the festivals?

Answer: This unfortunately is the type of question that is designed to shut down further discussion, instead of encouraging the searching for truth; however, there is an answer. In reference to the sins of Jeroboam, one of which was the changing of the feast days, Ellen White states, "The king's bold defiance of God in thus setting aside *divinely appointed institutions* was not allowed to pass unrebuked" (PK 101). Later in the book she states, "In the time of the end *every divine institution* is to be restored" (PK 678.2).

In *Patriarchs and Prophets*, Ellen White states, "Those who defer obedience till every shadow of uncertainty disappears and there remains no risk of failure or defeat, will never obey at all" (PP 290.2). Again, Ellen White states in the same book: "God will *never* remove every occasion for doubt. He gives sufficient evidence on which to base faith, and if this is not accepted, the mind is left in darkness" (PP 432.2).

Finally, she states in *The Great Controversy*, "While God has given ample evidence for faith, He will never remove all excuse for unbelief. All who look for hooks to hang their doubts upon will find them. And those who refuse to accept and obey God's word until every objection has been removed, and there is no longer an opportunity for doubt, will never come to the light" (GC 527.2).

There are better questions the theologian could have asked.

A. Are the feasts and statutes enjoined by God for worship? Yes! (See Lev. 23:1–44.)
B. Did Ellen White, in her writings separate the feasts from the rest of the statutes and deem them not applicable. No! (see "The Law of God" in the *Review and Herald*, May 6, 1875).
C. Did Ellen White ever refer to the feasts as laws? Yes! (see PP 311.3).
D. What did Ellen White call the feasts? *Divinely, appointed institutions* (see PK 101.3).
E. Did Ellen White ever prophesy that the feasts would be restored? Yes! (see PK 678.2).

Question 2: Is the Sabbath a *moed?*

Answer A: Yes! Leviticus 23:1–3 reads: "And the LORD spake unto Moses, saying, Speak unto the children of Israel, and say unto them, Concerning the *feasts* [H4150, *Moed*, "an appointment in time"] of the LORD, which ye shall proclaim to be *holy convocations* ["meeting," a rehearsal for heaven, H4744], even these are my feasts [H4150]. Six days shall work be done: but the seventh day is the sabbath of rest, an *holy convocation* [H4744]; ye shall do no work therein: it is the sabbath of the LORD in all your dwellings."

Answer B: It is also a holy convocation, as are the rest of the feasts.

Answer C: Ellen White describes the Sabbath as a feast [*moed*] in *The Great Controversy* when she quotes Henry Tuberville: " 'the very act of changing the Sabbath into Sunday, which Protestants allow of ... because by keeping Sunday, they acknowledge the church's power to ordain *feasts*, and to command them under sin.'— Henry Tuberville, *An Abridgment of the Christian Doctrine*, page 58" (GC 448.1).

Answer D: Ellen White connects the Sabbath with the rest of the feasts: "Again the people were reminded of the sacred obligation of the Sabbath. Yearly feasts were appointed, at which all the men of the nation were to assemble before the Lord, bringing to Him their offerings of gratitude and the first fruits of His bounties. The object of all these regulations was stated: they proceeded from no exercise of mere arbitrary sovereignty; all were given for the good of Israel. The Lord said, 'Ye shall be holy men unto Me'—worthy to be acknowledged by a holy God" (PP 311.2).

Question 3: What blessing would there be in keeping the feasts?

Answer A: You don't receive the curses or plagues (see Deut. 28:15–68).

Answer B: Ellen White states: "Strict compliance with the requirements of Heaven brings temporal as well as spiritual blessings" (PK 546.2).

Answer C: Ellen White states in *Prophets and Kings:* "God has in reserve a firmament of chosen ones that will yet shine forth amidst the darkness, revealing clearly to an apostate world the transforming power of obedience to His law" (PK 188.2).

Question 4: How are all the feasts eternal, when the spring feasts were fulfilled in Christ?

Note: This assertion is not true (see statements below).

Answer A1: "Christ, having eaten the Passover with His disciples, *instituted that feast* which was to commemorate His own death as 'the Lamb of God, which taketh away the sin of the world' " (GC 399.3).

Answer A2: "When the Saviour yielded up His life on Calvary, the significance of the Passover ceased, and the ordinance of the Lord's Supper was *instituted as a memorial* of the same event of which the Passover had been a type" (PP 539.5).

Answer B: Regarding Unleavened Bread, Ellen White states: "Paul says, in speaking of the resurrection of the Lord and of all His people: 'Christ the first fruits; afterward they that are Christ's at His coming.' 1 Corinthians 15:23. Like the wave sheaf, which was the first ripe grain gathered before the harvest, Christ is the first fruits of that immortal harvest of redeemed ones that at the *future resurrection shall be* gathered into the garner of God" (GC 399.2).

Answer C: Regarding Pentecost, Ellen White states: "In immediate connection with the scenes of the great day of God, the Lord by the prophet Joel has promised a special manifestation of His Spirit. Joel 2:28. This prophecy received a *partial fulfillment* in the outpouring of the Spirit on the Day of Pentecost; but it *will* reach its *full accomplishment* in the manifestation of divine grace *which will* attend the closing work of the gospel" (GC ix.3).

Answer D: The Bible states that six of the seven feasts are everlasting.

"And ye shall eat neither bread, nor parched corn, nor green ears, until the selfsame day that ye have brought an offering unto your God: it shall be *a statute for ever* throughout your generations in all your dwellings. ... And ye shall proclaim on the selfsame day, that it may be an holy convocation unto you: ye shall do no servile work therein: it shall be *a statute for ever* in all your dwellings throughout your generations. ... Ye shall do no manner of work: it shall be *a statute for ever* throughout your generations in all your dwellings. ... And ye shall keep it a feast unto the LORD seven days in the year. It shall be *a statute for ever* in your generations: ye shall celebrate it in the seventh month. ..." (Lev. 23:14, 21, 31, 41). "Wherefore the children of Israel shall keep the sabbath, to observe the sabbath throughout their generations, for *a perpetual covenant*" (Exod. 31:16).

The same Hebrew word is used to define "everlasting" (H5769) for both the covenant of the Sabbath and for the feasts (Exod. 31:16; Lev. 23:14, 21, 31, 41).

Answer E: The Bible states that the only feast which is not everlasting is Trumpets; which should give you pause to consider why. It has never had one fulfillment, yet. The historian's view of interpretation does not demand that there be only one fulfillment of a prophecy or type. None of the feasts have had their ultimate fulfillment. *Only the sacrifices* have met their ultimate fulfillment in Christ's sacrifice on the cross!

Question 5: How does a "festival" explain the Ten Commandments, as Ellen White states the statutes explain the Ten Commandments?

Answer A: The Lord's feast days are statutes—and most are *everlasting* statutes (see Lev. 23:14, 21, 31, 41, in Question #4, Answer D).

Answer B: The Lord's feast days are laws (see Ps. 81:4, 5; PP 311.2, 3).

Answer C: The Sabbath is a cornerstone of God's kingdom, and this is expounded upon by Paul in the book of Hebrews. Without the feast days, there is *no statute* to explain the Sabbath or the relationship God wants to establish with His people. *By doing away with the feasts, the church makes its own anti-Sabbath law!* And, by doing this, it gives credence to the precedent to *change* the Sabbath!

Answer D: "The *Catholic Church* not only abolished the Sabbath, but all the other Jewish festivals" (Bishop T. Enright, St. Louis, 1905).

Answer E: The Lord's feast days provide a timetable for the fulfillment of prophecy (see GC 399.4).

Answer F: The feast days and the seventh-day Sabbath are holy convocations (see Lev. 23:1–4). The word convocation [H4744] means "meeting" (a rehearsal for heaven). These days are symbolic of our life in heaven, and our acceptance of them is symbolic of our acceptance of the kingdom of heaven; and all the gifts and privileges that go with it. Jesus demonstrates this in His feast parables of the New Testament.

Answer G: Ellen White states: "*Again* the people were reminded of the *sacred obligation* of the *Sabbath*. Yearly feasts were appointed, at which all the men of the nation were to assemble before the Lord, bringing to Him their offerings of gratitude and the first fruits of His bounties. The object of all these regulations was stated: they proceeded from no exercise of mere arbitrary sovereignty; all were given for the good of Israel. The Lord said, 'Ye shall be holy men unto Me' [Exodus 22:31]—worthy to be acknowledged by a holy God. These *laws* were to be recorded by Moses, and carefully treasured as the *foundation* of the national law, and, *with* the ten precepts which they were given to illustrate, the condition of the fulfillment of God's promises to Israel" (PP 311.2, 3).

Question 6: Why do you say Jesus didn't keep the ceremonial law?

Answer A: I understand the reason for this question. Ever since the Catholic Church changed the Sabbath and the other feast days, almost every other church has followed suit to support the Catholic assertion that these holy convocations proclaimed by God are not necessary because they were nailed to the cross. Christ's keeping of the feasts but not the ceremonial law places the Jesuit idea that Scripture attacks other Scripture in jeopardy.

Ellen G. White states in *The Bible Echo*: "Christ passed through all the experiences of His childhood, youth, and manhood without the observance of ceremonial temple worship. He held no office, He assumed no rank. He passed through the experience of infancy, childhood, and manhood without a stain upon His character. He consecrated Himself to God that He might benefit and bless others, to show that in every period of life the human agent can do the Master's will" (*The Bible Echo*, Oct. 31, 1898, par. 7).

Note: Jesus passed through *childhood*, *youth* and *manhood* without the observance of the ceremonial temple worship, but He passed through the experience of "infancy, childhood, youth and manhood without a stain upon His character." What happened in Christ's infancy that involved ceremonial worship? Circumcision!

Answer B: Ellen White identifies the ceremonial law as "forms of worship to be maintained in the sanctuary" (PP 364.3). These forms had to do with "offerings" and "symbols pointing to Christ" (see also PK 684, 685, 687, 699, 705, 708; PP 364; 365.1; 367.2; DA 52.2; 608.1–2; *Review and Herald*, April 29, 1875, par. 2.)

Note: The reader is advised to read all of the statements referenced above. In no place are the feasts included with the ceremonial law (see Lev. 26:14, 15, 24, 25). *Also*, compare the above statements with her article in *Review and Herald*, May 6, 1875, which defines the law of God.

Question 7: Is circumcision part of the ceremonial law?

Yes! It took place in the temple and involved bloodletting. It has nothing to do with the moral law.

The circumcision that was performed on Christ was done to Him by His parents, in submission to the ceremonial law. This showed *their* obedience. Christ as child, youth and young man did not observe the ceremonial law, because He was spotless; He never sinned! The entire temple service, sacrifices, and offerings by fire have to do with sin!

Now that we have answered the pastor's questions, we will review the questions I gave to him.

Comment: Ellen White states this *fact*: "Saving faith is a transaction by which those who receive Christ join themselves in covenant relation with God. Genuine faith is life. A living faith means an increase of vigor, a confiding trust, by which the soul becomes a conquering power" (DA 347.1).

Comment: In Leviticus, God says, "But if ye will not hearken unto me, and will not do all these commandments; and if ye shall *despise my statutes*, or if your soul abhor my judgments, so that ye will not do *all* my commandments, but that ye break my *covenant*" (Lev. 26:14, 15).

Question 1: "Saving faith" is righteousness by faith. If righteousness by faith is a covenant relationship and this covenant can be broken by our rejection of God's statutes and judgments, does there remain an excuse for not keeping the statutes and judgments?

Comment: Ellen White uses Isaiah 24:1–8 in *Prophets and Kings* to speak of the great judgment day in which "the inspired messengers of Jehovah were given glimpses of the consternation of those unprepared to meet their Lord in peace. 'Behold, the Lord maketh the earth empty, and maketh it waste, and turneth it upside down, and scattereth abroad the inhabitants thereof; ... because they have transgressed the *laws* [*torah*, H8451], changed the *ordinance* ["statute," H2706], broken the everlasting covenant. Therefore hath the *curse* ["imprecation," H423] devoured the earth, and they that dwell therein are desolate.... The mirth of tabrets ceaseth, the noise of them that rejoice endeth, the joy of the harp ceaseth.' Isaiah 24:1–8" (PK 726; see also GC 657.1).

Question 2: In view of the above texts, which statutes have been changed?

Question 3: In view of the above texts, should we not endeavor keep *all* of God's statutes?

Question 4: If the statutes are not the "least of these commandments" in Matthew 5:19, what are?

Question 5: Does our obedience to the Catholic view of the feasts constitute placing the pope above God and obedience to man's law instead of God's Law? If not, why?

Comment: In an article entitled, "The Closing Work," Ellen White wrote the following:

"The saving knowledge of God will accomplish its purifying work on the mind and heart of every believer. The *Word* declares: 'Then will I sprinkle clean water upon you, and ye shall be clean: from all your filthiness, and from all your idols, will I cleanse you. A new heart also will I give you, and a new spirit will I put within you: and I will take away the stony heart out of your flesh, and I will give you an heart of flesh. And I will put my Spirit within you, and *cause you to walk in my statutes*.' [Ezekiel 36:25–27.] This is the descent of the Holy Spirit, sent from God to do its office work. The house of Israel is to be imbued with the Holy Spirit, and baptized with the grace of salvation" (*Review and Herald*, Oct. 13, 1904, par. 5).

Question 6: In view of the above statements, why are the feast statutes—especially the *everlasting* feast statutes—not included? Please include source(s).

Question 7: In view of the above statements, why is it acceptable to charge usury to church members for payment of their church loans and, when paid, the deed is returned to the conference? (See Ezek. 18:5–17.)

Comment: Paul in 1 Corinthians states: "Now these things were our *examples* ["types," G5179], ... Now all these things happened unto them for examples: and they are written for our *admonition* ["warning," G3559], upon whom the ends of the world are come" (1 Cor. 10:6, 11).

Ellen White states in *Patriarchs and Prophets*: "It was not His purpose that they should gain the land by warfare, but by strict obedience to His commands" (PP 392.3).

Question 8: In view of the two statements above and the fact that Adventists are not dispensationalists, why are Adventists exempted from all the statutes, judgments, and commandments as commanded in Leviticus 26:14–43?

Comment: "But if ye will not hearken unto me, and will not do all these commandments; and if ye shall despise my statutes, or if your soul abhor my judgments, so that ye will not do all my commandments, but that ye break my covenant" (Lev. 26:14, 15). "Then will I also walk contrary unto you, and will punish you yet seven times for your sins. And I will bring a sword upon you, that shall avenge the quarrel of my covenant: and when ye are gathered together within your cities, I will send the pestilence among you; and ye shall be delivered into the hand of the enemy" (Lev. 26:24, 25).

Question 9: How are Adventists and other Christians exempted from the *quarrel* ["vengeance," H5359] of His covenant? (see Lev. 26:25).

Question 10: Did Ellen White ever write another definitive exposition on the law that contradicted her May 6, 1875, article on the law? If not, why doesn't the church pay more attention to the original declaration she made?

Comment: "Ezra developed into a man of extraordinary learning and became a 'ready scribe in the law of Moses.' ... Ezra became a mouthpiece for God educating those about him in the *principles that govern heaven*. 'For Ezra had prepared his heart to seek the law of the LORD, and to do it, and to teach in Israel statutes and judgments.' [Ezra 7:10.]" (*Prophet and Kings*, p. 609.1, 2).

She adds, in *The Great Controversy:* "The Reformation had presented to the world an open Bible, unsealing the precepts of the law of God and urging its claims upon the consciences of the people. Infinite Love had unfolded to men the *statutes and principles of heaven*. God had said: 'Keep therefore and do them; for this is your wisdom and your *understanding* in the sight of the nations, which shall hear all these statutes, and say, Surely this great nation is a wise and understanding people.' Deuteronomy 4:6. When France rejected the gift of heaven, she sowed the seeds of anarchy and ruin; and the inevitable outworking of cause and effect resulted in the Revolution and the Reign of Terror" (GC 230.3).

> "Infinite Love had unfolded to men the statutes and principles of heaven."

Question 11: In view of these two statements, why does the Church reject the statutes that govern heaven?

Comment: In *Prophets and Kings*, Ellen White states: "In the closing work of God in the earth, the standard of His law will be again exalted" (PK 186.3).

"In consequence of continual transgression, the moral law was repeated in awful grandeur from Sinai. Christ gave to Moses religious precepts which were to govern the everyday life. These *statutes* were explicitly given to guard the ten commandments. They were not shadowy types to pass away with the death of Christ. They were to be *binding upon man in every age as long as time should last.* These commands were enforced by the power of the moral law, and they clearly and definitely explained that law" ("The Law of God," *Review and Herald*, May 6, 1875, par. 10).

Question 12: In view of the two statements above, is "the standard of God's law" that is "exalted," the one defined by Ellen White, which includes the statutes of God, or is it the one defined by Uriah Smith and G.I. Butler in 1888? Please give Bible texts and Spirit of Prophecy quotations to support your answer.

Question 13: If the answer to the question above omits the "everlasting statutes" of the feasts (see Leviticus 23); please state why, using Scriptural and Spirit of Prophecy quotations in your answer!

Regarding my answer to the theologian's *second* question #2; he stated in reply that Moses's statement in Leviticus 23, verses 1–3 was parenthetical. He had no reply to the other answers, and did not answer any of my following questions.

Catholic theologians have been telling us for hundreds of years that the common people are unable to interpret Scripture for himself and needs a theologian to tell him what Scripture means.

CHAPTER 17

OBEDIENCE—WORKS OR FAITH?

We don't work our way to heaven by our obedience; we only show God our loyalty to Him. We enter into God's rest.

"No works that the sinner can do will be efficacious in saving his soul. Obedience was always due to the Creator; for he endowed man with attributes for his service. God requires good works from man always; but good works cannot avail to earn salvation. It is impossible for man to save himself. He may deceive himself in regard to this matter; but he cannot save himself. Christ's righteousness alone can avail for his salvation, and this is the gift of God. This is the wedding garment prepared for you in which you may be a welcome guest at the marriage supper of the Lamb. Let faith take hold of Christ without delay, and you will be a new creature in Jesus, a light to the world" (*Review and Herald*, Dec. 20, 1892, par. 12).

> "We don't work our way to heaven by our obedience; we only show God our loyalty to Him."

The Progressive Nature of the Law

"Knowing this, that the law is not made for a righteous man, but for the lawless and disobedient, for the ungodly and for sinners, for unholy and profane, for murderers of fathers and murderers of mothers, for manslayers, for whoremongers, for them that defile themselves with mankind, for menstealers *[slave traders]*, for liars, for perjured persons *[perjurers]*, and if there be any other thing that is contrary to sound doctrine" (1 Tim. 1:9, 10).

1. **To receive God's blessings, we must keep His commandments.**

"And it shall come to pass, if thou shalt hearken diligently unto the voice of the LORD thy God, to observe and to do all his commandments which I command thee this day, that the LORD thy God will set thee on high above all nations of the earth: the LORD shall establish thee an holy people unto himself, as he hath sworn unto thee, if thou shalt keep the commandments of the LORD thy God, and walk in his ways. And the LORD shall make thee the head, and not the tail; and thou shalt be above only, and thou shalt not be beneath; if that thou hearken unto the commandments of the LORD thy God, which I command thee this day, to observe and to do them: and thou shalt not go aside from *any of the words which I command thee this day*, to the right hand, or to the left, to go after other gods to serve them" (Deut. 28:1, 9, 13, 14).

2. **To not receive the curses of God, we must observe and do all His commandments *and* His statutes.**

Notice that the commandments and statutes are listed together. "But it shall come to pass, if thou wilt not hearken unto the voice of the LORD thy God, to observe *to do all his commandments and his statutes* which I command thee this day; that all these curses shall come upon thee, and overtake thee: Moreover all these curses shall come upon thee, and shall pursue thee, and overtake thee, till thou be destroyed; because thou hearkenedst not unto the voice of the LORD thy God, to *keep his commandments and his statutes which he commanded* thee: If thou wilt not observe to do *all the words of this law that are written in this book*, that thou mayest fear this glorious and fearful name, THE LORD [*YEHOVAH*, H3068] THY GOD [*ELOHIYM*, H430]; then the LORD will make thy plagues wonderful, and the plagues of thy seed, even great plagues, and of long continuance, and sore sicknesses, and of long continuance" (Deut. 28:15, 45, 58, 59).

Note: There are similarities between the curses and some of the seven last plagues.

3. ***To be sanctified*, you must keep the Sabbath and the statutes.**

"And ye shall keep my statutes, and do them: I am the LORD which *sanctify* you" (Lev. 20:8).

"And I gave them *my statutes*, and shewed them *my judgments*, which if a man do, he shall even live in them. Moreover also I gave them *my sabbaths*, to be a sign between me and them, that they might know that I am the LORD that *sanctify* them. But the house of Israel rebelled against me in the wilderness: they walked not in *my statutes*, and they despised *my judgments*, which if a man do, he shall even live in them; and *my sabbaths* they greatly polluted" (Ezek. 20:11–13).

Regarding the statutes and judgments in Ezekiel 20, we are told:

" 'I am the Lord your God,' He said; 'walk in *My statutes*, and keep *My judgments*, and do them; and hallow *My Sabbaths*; and they shall be a sign between Me and you, that ye may know that I am the Lord your God.' In calling the attention of Judah to the sins that finally brought upon them the *Babylonian Captivity*, the Lord declared: 'Thou hast . . . profaned My Sabbaths.' 'Therefore have I poured out Mine indignation upon them; I have consumed them with the fire of My wrath: their own way have I recompensed upon their heads.' Ezekiel 20:19, 20; 22:8, 31" (PK 181.1–182.1).

"The closing words of Malachi are a prophecy regarding the work that should be done preparatory to the first and the second advent of Christ. This prophecy is introduced with the admonition, *'Remember ye the law of Moses my servant, which I commanded unto him in Horeb for all Israel, with the statutes and judgments. Behold, I will send you Elijah the prophet before the coming of the great and dreadful day of the Lord; and he shall turn the heart of the fathers to the children, and the heart of the children to their fathers, lest I come and smite the earth with a curse.'* [Malachi 4:4–6.]" (*The Southern Watchman*, March 21, 1905, par. 1, 2).

"In the visions of the prophets of old the Lord of glory was represented as bestowing special light upon His church in the days of darkness and unbelief preceding His second coming. As the Sun of Righteousness, He was to arise upon His church, 'with healing in His wings.' Malachi 4:2" (PK 716.3).

"In the closing work of God in the earth, the standard of His law will be again exalted" (PK 186.3).

Ellen G. White, in *The Great Controversy*, states that Malachi 3:5 describes the judgment, at the time of the end, including the statutes:

"Besides the coming of the Lord to His temple, Malachi also foretells His second advent, His coming for the execution of the judgment, in these words: 'And I will come near to you to judgment; and I will be a swift witness against the *sorcerers* [Lev. 19:31; Gal. 5:20, 21], and against the adulterers, and against *false swearers* [Lev. 19:12], and against *those that oppress* [Lev. 19:13; Exod. 22:21] the *hireling in his wages, the widow* [Deut. 10:18], and *the fatherless* [Deut. 14:29], and that *turn aside the stranger* [Deut. 24:19; 26:13] from his right, and fear not Me, saith the Lord of hosts.' Malachi 3:5" (GC 425.3).

Note: All the *emphasized* commands, in the text above, are *statutes*.

" 'Behold, the Lord maketh the earth empty, and maketh it waste, and turneth it upside down, and scattereth abroad the inhabitants thereof; . . . because they have transgressed the laws [*torah*, H8451, changed the ordinance (statute), broken the everlasting covenant. Therefore hath the curse ["imprecation," H423] devoured the earth, and they that dwell therein are desolate. . . . The mirth of tabrets ceaseth, the noise of them that rejoice endeth, the joy of the harp ceaseth.' Isaiah 24:1–8" (PK 726.2; see also GC 590, 657).

"Many do not hesitate to sneer at the word of God. Those who believe that word just as it reads are held up to ridicule. There is a growing contempt for law and order, directly traceable to a violation of the plain commands of Jehovah. Violence and crime are the result of turning aside from the path of obedience. Behold the wretchedness and misery of multitudes who worship at the shrine of idols and who seek in vain for happiness and peace" (PK 185.2).

"In the time of the end every divine institution is to be restored. The breach made in the law at the time the Sabbath was changed by man, is to be repaired. God's remnant people, standing before the world as reformers, are to show that the law of God is the foundation of all enduring reform and that the Sabbath of the fourth commandment is to stand as a memorial of creation, a constant reminder of the power of God. In clear, distinct lines they are to present the necessity of obedience to all the precepts of the Decalogue. Constrained by the love of Christ, they are to co-operate with Him in building up the waste places. They are to be repairers of the breach, restorers of paths to dwell in. [See Isaiah 58:12.]" (PK678.2).

"The saving knowledge of God will accomplish its purifying work on the mind and heart of every believer. The Word declares: 'Then will I sprinkle clean water upon you, and ye shall be clean: from all your filthiness, and from all your idols, will I cleanse you. A new heart also will I give you, and a new spirit will I put within you: and I will take away the stony heart out of your flesh, and I will give you an heart of flesh. And I will put my Spirit within you, and cause you to walk in my statutes.' *This is the descent of the Holy Spirit, sent from God to do its office work. The house of Israel is to be imbued with the Holy Spirit, and baptized with the grace of salvation*" (*Review and Herald*, Oct. 13, 1904, quoting Ezek. 36:25–27).

Biblical Examples of Laodicea

Don't be like the people who rejected the prophets in Scripture!

"Which of the prophets have not your fathers persecuted? and they have slain them which shewed before of the coming of the Just One; of whom ye have been now the betrayers and murderers: who have received the law by the disposition of angels, and have not kept it. Then they cried out with a loud voice, and *stopped their ears*, and ran upon him with one accord" (Acts 7:52, 53, 57).

"She *obeyed not the voice*; she received not correction; she trusted not in the LORD; she drew not near to her God" (Zeph. 3:2).

"This evil people, which refuse to hear my words, which walk in the *imagination* ["stubbornness," H8307] of their heart, and walk after other gods, to serve them, and to worship them, shall even be as this girdle, which is good for nothing. For as the girdle cleaveth to the loins of a man, so have I caused to cleave unto me the whole house of Israel and the whole house of Judah, saith the LORD; that they might be unto me for a people, and for a name, and for a praise, and for a glory: *but they would not hear*" (Jer. 13:10, 11).

"But *they obeyed not, neither inclined their ear*, but made their neck stiff, that they might not hear, nor receive instruction" (Jer. 17:23).

"I spake unto thee in thy prosperity; but thou saidst, I will not hear. This hath been thy manner from thy youth, that thou obeyedst not my voice" (Jer. 22:21).

"Neither will I any more remove the foot of Israel from out of the land which I have appointed for your fathers; so that they will take heed to do all that I have commanded them, according to the whole law and the statutes and the ordinances by the hand of Moses. And the LORD spake to Manasseh, and to his people: but *they would not hearken*" (2 Chron. 33:8, 10).

"Notwithstanding they *would not hear*, but hardened their necks, like to the neck of their fathers, that did not believe in the LORD their God. And they *rejected his statutes*, and his *covenant* that he made with their fathers ..." (2 Kings 17:14, 15; see Lev. 26:14–43; Deut. 28:15–68).

"Because they obeyed not the voice of the LORD their God, but transgressed his covenant, and all that Moses the servant of the LORD commanded, and *would not hear them, nor do them*" (2 Kings 18:12).

"And testifiedst against them, that thou mightest bring them again unto thy law: yet they dealt proudly, and *hearkened not* unto *thy commandments*, but *sinned against thy judgments*, (which if a man do, he shall live in them;)

and withdrew the shoulder, and hardened their neck, and *would not hear*" (Neh. 9:29).

"But they refused to hearken, and pulled away the shoulder, and *stopped their ears*, that they should not hear" (Zech. 7:11).

"Then shalt thou say unto them, Because your fathers have forsaken me, saith the LORD, and have walked after other gods, and have served them, and have worshipped them, and have forsaken me, and have not kept my law; and ye have done worse than your fathers; for, behold, ye walk every one after the imagination ["stubbornness," H8307] of his evil heart, that they may not hearken unto me" (Jer. 16:11, 12).

"And they *shall turn away their ears* from the truth, and shall be turned unto fables" (2 Tim. 4:4).

Jesus is calling Laodicea:

"Behold, I stand at the door, and knock: if any man *hear* my voice, and open the door, I will come in to him, and will sup ["have supper," G1172] with him, and he with me" (Rev. 3:20).

"… choose you this day whom ye will serve" (Joshua 24:15).

Jesus says, "I am the Alpha and the Omega …" (Rev. 1:8). "For I am the LORD, I change not…" (Mal. 3:6). "Jesus Christ the same yesterday, today and for ever" (Heb. 13:8).

God and His son, Jesus, are waiting for us to be totally obedient to His Word. Then, He will take us home.

Will you hear Jesus and invite Him in?

CHAPTER 18

THE SINS OF LAODICEA

"And he shall confirm the covenant with many for one week: and in the midst of the week he shall cause the sacrifice and the oblation to cease, and for the overspreading of abominations he shall make it desolate, even until the consummation, and that determined shall be poured upon the desolate" (Dan. 9:27).

What are the sins of Laodicea? The Bible gives us hints; study is necessary to find out. This is as God would have it, for, you see, Laodicea really doesn't want to know what its sins are. Much like Ephraim, it doesn't think it has any. In Hosea, we find Ephraim's assessment of itself: "...in all my labours they shall find none iniquity in me that were sin" (Hosea 12:8). We also find God's assessment of Ephraim: "Ephraim is joined to idols: let him alone" (Hosea 4:17). "When I would have healed Israel, then the iniquity of Ephraim was discovered ["denude," H1540]..." Hosea 7:1.

But, you say, it doesn't say that about Laodicea. Well, not exactly, but it does say that Laodicea is naked! "Because thou sayest, I am rich, and increased with goods, and have need of nothing; and knowest not that thou art wretched, and miserable, and poor, and blind, and *naked*" (Rev. 3:17).

In 2 Chronicles, there is mentioned a wicked king in Judah who made his people *naked*. "For the LORD brought Judah low because of Ahaz king of Israel; for he made Judah naked, and transgressed sore against the LORD. For he sacrificed unto the gods of Damascus, which smote him: and he said, Because the gods of the kings of Syria help them, therefore will I sacrifice to them, that they may help me. But they were the ruin of him, and of all Israel" (2 Chron. 28:19, 23).

Moses revealed the condition of *God's people* waiting at the foot of the mountain.

"And it came to pass, as soon as he came nigh unto the camp, that he saw the calf, and the dancing: and Moses' anger waxed hot, and he cast the tables out of his hands, and brake them beneath the mount. ... And when Moses saw that the people were *naked*; (*for Aaron had made them naked unto their shame among their enemies:*) Then Moses stood in the gate of the camp, and said, Who is on the LORD's side? let him come unto me. And all the sons of Levi gathered themselves together unto him" (Exod. 32:19, 25, 26).

Note: When the Bible describes groups of people naked, it is referring to idol worship.

In Revelation, Jesus says: "Because thou sayest, I am rich, and increased with goods, and have need of nothing; and knowest not that thou art wretched, and miserable, and poor, and blind, and *naked:* I counsel thee to buy of me gold tried in the fire, that thou mayest be rich; and white raiment, that thou mayest be clothed, and that the shame of thy nakedness do not appear; and anoint thine eyes with eyesalve, that thou mayest see" (Rev. 3:17, 18).

So you see (or maybe you do not if you are Laodicea), Laodicea is not only naked, like the people in the time of Ahaz and Moses, but they are also blind like the Pharisees in the time of Christ and, like those men, they think they can see.

"And Jesus said, For judgment I am come into this world, that they which see not might see; and that they which see might be made blind. And some of the Pharisees which were with him heard these words, and said unto him, Are we blind also? Jesus said unto them, If ye were blind, ye should have no sin: but now ye say, We see; therefore your sin remaineth" (John 9:39–41).

> Much like Laodicea, Jesus had come unto the Pharisees who had a much different idea of themselves than Christ did. This is the result of sin in our lives. It makes us blind to our own sins and very much aware of the sins of others.

Much like Laodicea, Jesus had come unto the Pharisees who had a much different idea of themselves than Christ did. This is the result of sin in our lives. It makes us blind to our own sins and very much aware of the sins of others.

Jesus goes on to talk about the dangers of blindness, for sheep that do not see are prone to follow a thief or robber who does not enter by the door into the sheep fold. "But he that entereth in by the door is the shepherd of the sheep. To him the porter openeth; and the sheep hear his voice: and he calleth his own sheep by name, and leadeth them out. And when he putteth forth his own sheep, he goeth before them, and the sheep follow him: for they know his voice. And a stranger will they not follow, but will flee from him: for they know not the voice of strangers" (John 10:2–5).

"As many as I love, I rebuke and chasten: be zealous therefore, and repent" (Rev. 3:19).

Jesus says, "Behold, I stand at the door, and knock: if any man hear my voice, and open the door, I will come in to him, and will sup with him, and he with me" (Rev. 3:20).

So, just like Ephraim, who doesn't think it has any sin, and the naked Israelites at the foot of Mount Sinai, and the idolatrous subjects of Ahaz, *Laodicea is naked*.

Well, what do these four groups have in common? They are all idolaters. *This is why Laodicea is naked*.

By the way, *who has made Laodicea naked?*

Who else is naked in Revelation? The whore who gets burned with fire: "And the ten horns which thou sawest upon the beast, these shall hate the whore, and shall make her desolate and naked, and shall eat her flesh, and burn her with fire" (Rev. 17:16).

There are no statues; there are no golden idols to burn incense to, but there is idolatry. What is the idol in Laodicea's heart?

If we look in Scripture, maybe we can find out.

Paul describes covetousness as idolatry.

"Mortify therefore your members which are upon the earth; fornication, uncleanness, inordinate affection, evil concupiscence, and *covetousness*, which *is idolatry*" (Col. 3:5). "For this ye know, that no whoremonger, nor unclean person, nor *covetous man*, who *is an idolater*, hath any inheritance in the kingdom of Christ and of God" (Eph. 5:5).

In 1 Samuel, the prophet describes and defines idolatry: "For rebellion is as the sin of witchcraft, and *stubbornness is as iniquity* and *idolatry*. *Because thou hast rejected the word of the LORD*, he hath also rejected thee from being king" (1 Sam. 15:23).

Note: The stubborn rejection of the word of the Lord is as iniquity and idolatry.

Jeremiah compares serving other gods and forsaking *God's law* and *not keeping them* with walking in the imagination ["stubbornness," H8307] of his evil heart. "Then shalt thou say unto them, Because your fathers have forsaken me, saith the LORD, and have walked after other gods, and have served them, and have worshipped them, and have forsaken me, and have not kept my law; and ye have done worse than your fathers; for, behold, ye walk every one after the imagination ["stubbornness," H8307] of his evil heart, that they may not hearken unto me" (Jer. 16:11, 12).

Moses states: "And ye have seen their abominations, and their idols, wood and stone, silver and gold, which were among them:) Lest there should be among you man, or woman, or family, or tribe, whose heart turneth away this day from the LORD our God, to go and serve the gods of these nations; lest there should be among you a root that beareth gall and wormwood; and it come to pass, when he heareth the words of this curse ["imprecation," H423], that he bless himself in his heart, saying, I shall have peace, though I walk in the imagination ["stubbornness," H8307] of mine heart, to add drunkenness to thirst" (Deut. 29:17–19).

"It is as easy to make an idol of cherished ideas or objects as to fashion gods of wood or stone. Thousands have a false conception of God and His attributes. They are as verily serving a false God as were the servants of Baal" (5T 173.4).

How do we, as Seventh-day Adventists, describe ourselves? We use Revelation 12: "And there appeared a great wonder in heaven; a woman clothed with the sun, and the moon under her feet, and upon her head a crown of twelve stars: and the dragon was wroth with the woman, and went to make war with the *remnant of her seed*, which keep the commandments of God, and have *the testimony* of Jesus Christ" (Rev. 12:1, 17).

How does God and the Elijah he sent to us describe us? "Because thou sayest, I am rich, and increased with goods, and have need of nothing; and knowest not that thou art wretched, and miserable, and poor, and blind, and naked" (Rev. 3:17).

How can we reconcile these two views of ourselves?
There are two *naked women* in *Revelation*: Laodicea and the whore. We have read what it says regarding Laodicea. Regarding the whore, Revelation states: "And the ten horns which thou sawest upon the beast, these shall hate the whore, and shall make her desolate and naked, and shall eat her flesh, and burn her with fire" (Rev. 17:16).

The *ten horns hate the whore* and shall make her desolate and naked; but Scripture doesn't tell us who has made Laodicea naked.

All other groups described in Scripture as naked were idolaters. *Whether we worship the god of our own ideas and stubbornness or bow to an image we have made, it makes no difference—we are idolaters.*

Laodicea *will* worship the image to the beast because she is an idolater. *Yet, we don't have to worship the image*. Follow Jesus, walk in His footsteps, and obey His every command, and He will give you the gift of His Spirit.

Jesus said, "Remember Lot's wife" (Luke 17:32). As we move on toward the end of time, it's important that we remember these words of Jesus. Lot was told by the angels not to look back toward Sodom; there was and is nothing there. Accept what the Bible tells us; pray as you make your decisions to be obedient *to everything* God has told us in His Word, and Jesus will guide you safely home.

Do you ever wonder what the people of Sodom thought as they saw righteous Lot leave their town that day? Did they, like Pharaoh, defy the God of heaven saying, "Who is God that we should obey Him?" Or did they, like the Pharisees of Christ's day, say that this man has a demon, ascribing the works of God to the devil and thereby committing the unpardonable sin?

Perhaps they, like Jehoiakim, cut up Lot's writings as he left town and burnt them, warming themselves in the heat of the fire.

They might have, even like Felix, said that Lot had almost convinced them to believe and that, when he got back, they were going to listen to him and change their ways.

You see it doesn't really matter, does it? It really doesn't count for anything, in God's book of our life, why we reject what He wants us to learn. It doesn't matter to those Jews who rejected Christ that He cried for them as He walked toward the Mount of Olives.

In Isaiah, God tells us, "For I will not contend for ever, neither will I be always wroth: for the *spirit should fail* before me, and the souls which I have made. For the iniquity of his covetousness was I wroth, and smote him: I hid me, and was wroth, and he went on frowardly in the way of his heart" (Isa. 57:16, 17).

> " It really doesn't count for anything, in God's book of our life, why we reject what He wants us to learn. "

Obedience Declares Faith

In the Old and New Testaments, we are called to be a peculiar people.

"But ye are a chosen generation, a royal priesthood, an holy nation, a peculiar people; that ye should shew forth the praises of him who hath called you out of darkness into his marvellous light" (1 Peter 2:9).

"This day the LORD thy God hath commanded thee to do these statutes and judgments: thou shalt therefore keep and do them with all thine heart, and with all thy soul. Thou hast avouched the LORD this day to be thy God, and to walk in his ways, and to keep his statutes, and his commandments, and his judgments, and to hearken unto his voice: and the LORD hath avouched thee this day to be his peculiar people, as he hath promised thee, and that thou shouldest keep all his commandments" (Deut. 26:16–18).

Several years ago, now, I and my wife decided to do something "radical"—to take God at His word and commit to keeping all of God's statutes, judgments, precepts, commandments, laws and testimonies beginning at what we knew. It was experimental religion. "O taste and see that the LORD is good: blessed is the man that trusteth in him" (Ps. 34:8). We have never been happier or more blessed in all our lives and in whatever we have undertaken. We have never wanted to go back to what we didn't have.

Won't you give it a try? Won't you, *by faith*, give God the true obedience He asks for? He will work in you both to will and to accomplish His good pleasure, and "fulfil all the good pleasure of his goodness, and the work of faith with power: that the name of our Lord Jesus Christ may be glorified in you, and ye in him, according to the grace of our God and the Lord Jesus Christ" (2 Thess. 1:11, 12). The alternatives are not good!

"Christ was obedient to every requirement of the law. He said of Himself, 'I delight to do Thy will, O My God; yea, Thy law is within My heart.' Psalm 40:8. When on earth, He said to His disciples, 'I have kept My Father's commandments.' John 15:10. *By His perfect obedience He has made it possible for every human being to obey God's commandments.* When we submit ourselves to Christ, the heart is united with His heart, the will is merged in His will, the mind becomes one with His mind, the thoughts are brought into captivity to Him; we live His life. This is what it means to be clothed with the garment of His righteousness. Then as the Lord looks upon us He sees, not the fig-leaf garment, not the nakedness and deformity of sin, but His own robe of righteousness, which is perfect obedience to the law of Jehovah. ... Righteousness is right doing, and it is by their deeds that all will be judged. Our characters are revealed by what we do. The works show whether the faith is genuine. ... 'He that keepeth His commandments dwelleth in Him, and He in him. And hereby we know that He abideth in us, by the Spirit which He hath given us.' 'Hereby we do know that we know Him if we keep His commandments.' 1 John 3:24; 1 John 2:3. This is the genuine evidence of conversion. Whatever our profession, it amounts to nothing unless Christ is revealed in works of righteousness" (COL 311.4–312.3, emphasis added).

"He that turneth away his ear from hearing the law [*torah*], even his prayer shall be abomination" (Prov. 28:9).

"God has placed in His word no *command* which men may obey or disobey at will and not suffer the consequences. If men choose any other path than that of strict obedience, they will find that 'the end thereof are the ways of death.' Proverbs 14:12" (PP 360).

"To the very close of the controversy in heaven the great usurper continued to justify himself. When it was announced that with all his sympathizers he must be expelled from the abodes of bliss, then the rebel leader boldly avowed his contempt for the Creator's law. He reiterated his claim that angels needed no control, but should be left to follow their own will, which would ever guide them right. He denounced the *divine statutes* as a restriction of their liberty and declared that it was his purpose to secure the abolition of law; that, freed from this restraint, the hosts of heaven might enter upon a more exalted, more glorious state of existence" (GC 499.2).

"Says the Scripture, 'Forever, O Lord, Thy word is settled in heaven.' 'All His commandments are sure. They stand fast forever and ever.' Psalm 119:89; 111:7, 8. The *sacred statutes* which Satan has hated and sought to destroy, will be honored throughout a sinless universe" (PP 342.2, emphasis added).

"…when God's judgments shall fall upon the earth before its deluge by fire, the impenitent will know just where and what their sin is—the despising of His holy law" (PP 99.3).

We have arrived back from where we started—in Daniel 9:27. Jesus, with His atonement for our sins, has caused the sacrifice ["slaughter," H2077] and the oblation ["meat offering," H4503] to cease. "For the overspreading of abominations ["filthiness," H8251] he shall make it desolate ["to make numb," H8074], even until the consummation, and that determined shall be poured upon the desolate ["ruined," H8076 (from H8074; sins make us numb to its effects on us)]." Have you grown numb to the sin in your life? *It's time to wake up; Jesus is coming soon!*

CHAPTER 19

THE WAY IS THE OLD WAY

In *The Great Controversy*, Ellen White wrote to God's professed people regarding the future, quoting Jeremiah:

"It is only as the law of God is restored to its rightful position that there can be a revival of primitive faith and godliness among His professed people. '*Thus saith the Lord, Stand ye in the ways, and see, and ask for the old paths, where is the good way, and walk therein, and ye shall find rest for your souls.*' Jeremiah 6:16" (GC 478.3).

In *Prophets and Kings*, she comments on the *same verse* in this way, regarding the foundation of faith in the Old Testament: "*Jeremiah called their attention repeatedly to the counsels given in Deuteronomy. More than any other of the prophets, he emphasized the teachings of the Mosaic law and showed how these might bring the highest spiritual blessing to the nation and to every individual heart. 'Ask for the old paths, where is the good way, and walk therein,' he pleaded, 'and ye shall find rest for your souls.'* Jeremiah 6:16" (PK 411.1).

Ellen G. White uses this text to define the foundations of faith:

"*Thus saith the Lord, Stand ye in the ways, and see, and ask for the old paths, where is the good way, and walk therein*. Jeremiah 6:16. Let none seek to tear away the foundations of our faith—the foundations that were laid at the beginning of our work by prayerful study of the word and by revelation. Upon these foundations we have been building for the last fifty years. Men may suppose that they have found a new way and that they can lay a stronger foundation than that which has been laid. But this is a great deception. Other foundation can no man lay than that which has been laid. In the past many have undertaken the building of a new faith, the establishment of new principles. But how long did their building stand? It soon fell, for it was not founded upon the Rock" (8T 296.3–297.2).

Will we respond as God's remnant people or will we, like the Jews, respond as they did in the last sentence of this verse: "But they said, *We will not walk therein*" (Jer. 6:16).

"In these last days there is a call from Heaven inviting *you to keep the statutes* and ordinances of the Lord. The world has set at naught the law of Jehovah; but God will not be left without a witness to his righteousness, or without a people in the earth to proclaim his truth" (*Signs of the Times*, Feb. 3, 1888, par. 5).

"The saving knowledge of God will accomplish its purifying work on the mind and heart of every believer. The Word declares: 'Then will I sprinkle clean water upon you, and ye shall be clean: from all your filthiness, and from all your idols, will I cleanse you. A new heart also will I give you, and a new spirit will I put within you: and I will take away the stony heart out of your flesh, and I will give you an heart of flesh. *And I will put my Spirit within you, and cause you to walk in my statutes.*' [Ezek. 36:25–27.] *This is the descent of the Holy Spirit, sent from God to do its office work. The house of Israel is to be imbued with the Holy Spirit, and baptized with the grace of salvation*" ("The Closing Work," *Review and Herald*, Oct. 13, 1904, par. 5).

God is calling to His church to repent and keep all His law!

"My people are destroyed for lack of knowledge: because thou hast rejected knowledge, I will also reject thee, that thou shalt be no priest to me: seeing thou hast forgotten the law [*torah*] of thy God, I will also forget thy children" (Hosea 4:6).

"I have written to him the great things of my law [*torah*], but they were counted as a strange thing" (Hosea 8:12).

"Therefore have I also made you contemptible and base before all the people, according as ye have not kept my ways, but have been partial in the law [*torah*]" (Mal. 2:9).

Have we become contemptible because we have been partial in the law? Has the law [*torah*] become a strange thing to God's church? Are we being destroyed for a lack of knowledge because we have forgotten the law of God?

"When their children should ask in time to come, 'What mean the testimonies, and the statutes, and the judgments, which the Lord our God hath commanded you?' then the parents were to repeat the history of

God's gracious dealings with them—how the Lord had wrought for their deliverance that they might obey His Law—and to declare to them, 'The Lord commanded us to do all these statutes, to fear the Lord our God, for our good always, that He might preserve us alive, as it is at this day. And it shall be our righteousness, if we observe to do all these commandments before the Lord our God as He hath commanded us' [Deut. 6:24, 25]" (PP 468.2).

"The infinite love of God has been manifested in the gift of His only-begotten Son to redeem a lost race. Christ came to the earth to reveal to men the character of His Father, and His life was filled with deeds of divine tenderness and compassion. And yet Christ Himself declares, 'Till heaven and earth pass, one jot or one tittle shall in no wise pass from the law.' Matthew 5:18. *The same voice that with patient, loving entreaty invites the sinner to come to Him and find pardon and peace, will in the judgment bid the rejecters of His mercy, 'Depart from Me, ye cursed* [imprecation].' Matthew 25:41. In all the Bible, God is represented not only as a tender father but as a righteous judge. Though He delights in showing mercy, and 'forgiving iniquity and transgression and sin,' yet He 'will by no means clear the guilty.' Exodus 34:7" (PP 469.2).

"Every chapter and every verse of the Bible is a communication from God to men. We should bind its precepts as signs upon our hands and as frontlets between our eyes. 'And thou shalt bind them for a sign upon thine hand, and they shall be as frontlets between thine eyes.' Deuteronomy 6:8. If studied and obeyed, it would lead God's people, as the Israelites were led, by the pillar of cloud by day and the pillar of fire by night" (PP 504.3).

"As you receive the word in faith, it will give you power to obey" (MB 150.1).

God bless you, brother and sister, as you consider what God has asked us to do.

CHAPTER 20

REBELLION

Definition of "Rebel"

"It is not the greatness of the act of disobedience that constitutes sin, but the fact of variance from God's expressed will in the least particular; for this shows that there is yet communion between the soul and sin. The heart is divided in its service. There is a virtual denial of God, a rebellion against the laws of His government" (MB 51.3).

"Whenever men choose their own way, they place themselves in controversy with God. They will have no place in the kingdom of heaven, for they are at war with the very principles of heaven. In disregarding the will of God, they are placing themselves on the side of Satan, the enemy of God and man. Not by one word, not by many words, but by every word that God has spoken, shall man live. We cannot disregard one word, however trifling it may seem to us, and be safe. There is not a commandment of the law that is not for the good and happiness of man, both in this life and in the life to come. In obedience to God's law, man is surrounded as with a hedge and kept from the evil. He who breaks down this divinely erected barrier at one point has destroyed its power to protect him; for he has opened a way by which the enemy can enter to waste and ruin" (MB 52.1).

Rebellion is:

1. A refusal to believe God (Num. 13:1, 31; 14:9) ["to rebel" (prime root, exact meaning), H4775].
2. To resist against the commandment(s) of the Lord. ["to resist" (prime root), H4784]. "Whosoever he be that doth *rebel* against thy

commandment, and will not hearken unto thy words in all that thou commandest him, he shall be put to death: only be strong and of a good courage" (Joshua 1:18).
3. People who know Him and not see His days. "Why, seeing times are not hidden from the Almighty, do they that know him not see his days? They are of those that *rebel* [H4775] against the light; they know not the ways thereof, nor abide in the paths thereof" (Job 24:1, 13).
4. The contrast is between those who are "willing and obedient" and blessed and those who *refuse* ["refuse" (prime root), H3985] and *rebel* ["to resist," H4784] and are *devoured* ["consumed," H398]. "Come now, and let us reason together, saith the LORD: though your sins be as scarlet, they shall be as white as snow; though they be red like crimson, they shall be as wool. If ye be willing and obedient, ye shall eat the good of the land: but if ye *refuse* and *rebel*, ye shall be devoured with the sword: for the mouth of the LORD hath spoken it" (Isa. 1:18–20).
5. *Those who rebel* have fled from God: "*Destruction* [H7701] unto them." "Woe unto them! for they have fled from me: destruction unto them! because they have *transgressed* ["break away from just authority," H6586] against me: though I have redeemed them, yet they have spoken lies against me ... and they rebel against me" (Hosea 7:13, 14).
6. *Rebellion* ["to resist," H4784] involves not believing Him, *listening* ["hearing," H8085] to Him, or hearkening unto Him. "Likewise when the LORD sent you from Kadeshbarnea, saying, Go up and possess the land which I have given you; then ye rebelled against the commandment of the LORD your God, and ye believed him not, nor hearkened to his voice. Ye have been rebellious against the LORD from the day that I knew you" (Deut. 9:23, 24).

In defining rebellion, Paul quotes David who quotes Moses.

Hebrews 3:7–11, 15, 19 – "Wherefore (as the Holy Ghost saith, To day if ye will hear his voice, harden not your hearts, as in the provocation, in the day of temptation in the wilderness: when your fathers tempted me, proved me, and saw my works forty years. Wherefore I was grieved with that generation, and said, They do alway err in their heart; and *they have not known my ways*. So I sware in my wrath, They shall not enter into my rest.) While it is said, To day if ye will hear his voice, harden not your hearts, as in the provocation. So we see that they could not enter in because of unbelief."

Hebrews 4:7 – "Again, he limiteth a certain day, saying in David, To day, after so long a time; as it is said, To day if ye will hear his voice, harden not your hearts."

Psalm 95:7–11 – "For he is our God; and we are the people of his pasture, and the sheep of his hand. To day if ye will hear his voice, harden not your heart, as in the provocation, and as in the day of temptation in the wilderness: when your fathers tempted me, proved me, and saw my work. Forty years long was I grieved with this generation, and said, It is a people that do err in their heart, and they have not known *my ways*: unto whom I sware in my wrath that they should not enter into my rest."

Psalm 81:7, 8, 11–13 – "Thou calledst in trouble, and I delivered thee; I answered thee in the secret place of thunder: I proved thee at the waters of Meribah. Selah. Hear, O my people, and I will testify unto thee: O Israel, if thou wilt hearken unto me; but my people would not hearken to my voice; and Israel would none of me. So I gave them up unto their own hearts' lust [H8307, stubborness]: and they walked in their own counsels. Oh that my people had hearkened unto me, and Israel had walked in my ways!"

Deuteronomy 6:16, 17 – "Ye shall not tempt the LORD your God, as ye tempted him in Massah. Ye shall diligently keep the commandments of the LORD your God, and his testimonies, and his statutes, which he hath commanded thee."

Exodus 17:7 – "And he called the name of the place Massah, and Meribah, because of the chiding of the children of Israel, and because they tempted the LORD, saying, Is the LORD among us, or not?" [Doubt, when God has given ample evidence.]

Deuteronomy 9:22–24 – "And at Taberah, and at Massah, and at Kibrothhattaavah, ye provoked the LORD to wrath. Likewise when the LORD sent you from Kadeshbarnea, saying, Go up and possess the land which I have given you; then ye *rebelled against the commandment of the LORD your God*, and *ye believed him not, nor hearkened to his voice*. Ye have been rebellious against the LORD from the day that I knew you."

Numbers 20:13, 24 – "This is the water of Meribah; because the children of Israel strove with the LORD, and he was sanctified in them. Aaron shall be gathered unto his people: for he shall not enter into the land which I have given unto the children of Israel, because ye *rebelled against my word [mouth]* at the water of Meribah."

Rebellion at the End of Time

Hosea 8:1–3, 12 – "Set the trumpet to thy mouth. He shall come as an eagle against the house of the LORD, because they [the lost] have transgressed my covenant, and trespassed against my law. Israel shall cry unto me, *My God, we know thee.* Israel hath cast off the thing that is good: the enemy shall pursue him. *I have written to him the great things of my law, but they were counted as a strange thing.*"

How does Ellen White describe rebellion?

Ellen White outlines the nature of rebellion and its source: "In the condition of the world that existed before the Flood they saw illustrated the results of the administration which Lucifer had endeavored to establish in heaven, in rejecting the authority of Christ and casting aside the law of God. In those high-handed sinners of the antediluvian world they saw the subjects over whom Satan held sway. The thoughts of men's hearts were only evil continually. Genesis 6:5. Every emotion, every impulse and imagination, was at war with the divine principles of purity and peace and love. It was an example of the awful depravity resulting from *Satan's policy to remove* from God's creatures the restraint of His holy law" (PP 78.4).

"Satan was urging upon men the belief that there was no reward for the righteous or punishment for the wicked, and that it was impossible for men to obey the divine statutes. But in the case of Enoch, God declares 'that He is, and that He is a rewarder of them that diligently seek Him.' Hebrews 11:6. He shows what He will do for those who keep His commandments. Men were taught that it is possible to obey the law of God; that even while living in the midst of the sinful and corrupt, they were able, by the grace of God, to resist temptation, and become pure and holy. ... The godly character of this prophet represents the state of holiness which *must* be attained by those who shall be 'redeemed from the earth' (Revelation 14:3) at the time of Christ's second advent. ... But like Enoch, God's people will seek for purity of heart and conformity to His will, until they shall reflect the likeness of Christ. Like Enoch, they will warn the world of the Lord's second coming and of the judgments to be visited upon transgression, and by their holy conversation and example they will condemn the sins of the ungodly" (PP 88.2, 3, emphasis added).

Again, she writes concerning the cause and the results of rebellion: "The Lord had declared to Israel, 'Ye shall not do ... every man whatsoever is right in his own eyes;' but ye shall 'observe and hear all these words which I command thee.' Deuteronomy 12:8, 28. [Note from which chapter she quotes.] In deciding upon any course of action we are not to ask whether we can see that harm will result from it, but whether it is in keeping with the will of God. 'There is a way which seemeth right unto a man; but the end thereof are the ways of death' (Prov. 14:12)" (PP 634.2).

"Yet with the sin of Saul and its result before us, how many are pursuing a similar course. While they refuse to believe and obey some *requirement* of the Lord, they persevere in offering up to God their formal services of religion. There is no response of the Spirit of God to such service. No matter how zealous men may be in their observance of religious ceremonies, the Lord cannot accept them if they persist in willful violation of one of His commands.

" 'Rebellion is as the sin of witchcraft, and stubbornness is as iniquity and idolatry.' Rebellion originated with Satan, and all rebellion against God is directly due to satanic influence. Those who set themselves *against the government of God* have entered into an alliance with the archapostate, and he will exercise his power and cunning to captivate the senses and mislead the understanding. He will cause everything to appear in a false light. Like our first parents, those who are under his bewitching spell see only the great benefits to be received by transgression.

"No stronger evidence can be given of Satan's delusive power than that many who are thus led by him deceive themselves with the belief that they are in the service of God. When *Korah*, *Dathan*, and *Abiram* rebelled against the authority of Moses, they thought they were opposing only a human leader, a man like themselves; and they came to believe that they were verily doing God service. But in rejecting God's chosen instrument they rejected Christ; they insulted the Spirit of God. So, in the days of Christ, the *Jewish scribes* and *elders*, who professed great zeal for the honor of God, crucified His Son. The *same spirit still exists* in the hearts of those who set themselves to follow their own will in opposition to the will of God.

"It is a perilous step to slight the reproofs and warnings of God's word or of His Spirit. Many, like Saul, yield to temptation until they become blind to the true character of sin. They flatter themselves that they have had some good object in view, and have done no wrong in departing from the Lord's *requirements*. Thus they do despite to the Spirit of grace, until its voice is no longer heard, and *they are left to the delusions which they have chosen*" (PP 634.2–635.4).

Questions for the Bible Student

Question: Are those who set themselves *"against the government of God"* rebelling against the principles that govern heaven? (see PK 570.2; 609.1, 2; 677.1, 3; 20.1; GC 230.3; PP 311.2, 3).

In an effort to point out the absurdity of obeying all the statutes, a Seventh-day Adventist pastor recently asked me if a small law ["the least of these"] in Leviticus 19:27 was still binding and needed to be obeyed, that of not shaving off the corner of one's beard (Lev. 21:5). I replied that I didn't wear a beard, and I thought no more of the question, but I wonder now if the pastor had not nailed down the very crux of the difference between us?

> **Question 1**—Who gets to decide if one portion of Scripture is dated or absurd and doesn't need to be followed or obeyed?
>
> **Question 2**—If that person is someone in the Church [like my friend the pastor], where does the power stop?
>
> **Question 3**—Isn't that what the Catholic pope has done and continues to do in setting himself up as the arbiter of truth?
>
> **Question 4**—Are we ourselves attempting to be arbiters of truth, accepting from Scripture what *we see* as truth?
>
> **Question 5**—Is the Church or the government the arbiter of truth?

I have not supplied answers to the questions above because each of us must answer these questions.

Ellen White wrote in *Patriarchs and Prophets:* "*Every chapter* and *every verse* of the Bible is a communication from God to men. We should bind its precepts as signs upon our hands and as frontlets between our eyes. If studied and obeyed, it would lead God's people, as the Israelites were led, by the pillar of cloud by day and the pillar of fire by night" (PP 504.3).

Scripture is either the Word of God or it isn't.
See 2 Timothy 3:16, 17; Deuteronomy 29:29; *Patriarchs and Prophets*, p. 73, par. 2; 360, par. 2.)

Although the central ideas of natural law have been part of Christian thought since the Roman Empire, the foundation for natural law was laid by *Thomas Aquinas* as he synthesized ideas from his predecessors and condensed them into his "Lex Naturalis," or Natural Law (see Jacques Maritain, *Les Droits de l'Homme et la Loi Naturelle* ["The Rights of Man and Natural Law"], 1942). St. Thomas believed reason was a part of divinity in man. Non-fundamentalist Christians—especially Catholics—believe that our reason is unfallen. However, this belief is at odds with biblical thinking and the Scriptures. If scriptural interpretation is in any way dependent upon our fallen reasoning, then man becomes the arbiter of what truth is. The doctrine, or concept, of natural law is pervasive in our society, whether or not it is taught by Jesuits as a course or as just the way modern people—especially educated ones—think. The following statements are what the Bible itself says about human reasoning.

> "If scriptural interpretation is in any way dependent upon our fallen reasoning, then man becomes the arbiter of what truth is."

1. "I had not known sin, but by the law." (Rom. 7:7).
2. "There is a way which seemeth right unto a man, but the end thereof are the ways of death." (Prov. 14:12)
3. "Every way of a man is right in his own eyes: but the LORD pondereth the hearts." (Prov. 21:2)
4. "Woe unto them that are wise in their own eyes, and prudent in their own sight!" (Isa. 5:21)
5. "In those days there was no king in Israel, but every man did that which was right in his own eyes." (Judges 17:6)
6. "Ye shall not do after all [the things] that we do here this day, every man whatsoever [is] right in his own eyes." (Deut. 12:8)
7. "The way of a fool is right in his own eyes: but he that hearkeneth unto counsel is wise." (Prov. 12:15)
8. "And, behold, a certain lawyer stood up, and tempted him, saying, Master, what shall I do to inherit eternal life? He said unto him, What is written in the law? how readest thou?" (Luke 10:25, 26)
  Note: Jesus did not ask his opinion on anything except the above-mentioned two things, neither of which required reasoning to answer.

"God has not made the reception of the gospel to depend upon human reasoning. ... The gospel is the power of God and the wisdom of God. .... The word is to be respected and obeyed. That book which contains the record of *Christ's life, his work, his doctrines, his sufferings, and final triumphs*, is to be the source of our strength. " (YI, Oct. 13, 1898, par. 10, 11)

In the chapter, "The Scriptures a Safeguard," in *The Great Controversy*, Ellen White wrote: "Many a portion of Scripture which learned men pronounce a mystery, or pass over as unimportant, is full of comfort and instruction to him who has been taught in the school of Christ. One reason why many theologians have no clearer understanding of God's word is, *they close their eyes to truths which they do not wish to practice.* An understanding of Bible truth depends not so much on the power of intellect brought to the search as on the singleness of purpose, the earnest longing after righteousness" (GC 599.2).

"The language of the Bible should be explained according to its *obvious meaning*, unless a symbol or figure is employed. Christ has given the promise: 'If any man will do His will, he shall know of the doctrine.' John 7:17. If men would but take the Bible as it reads, if there were no false teachers to mislead and confuse their minds, a work would be accomplished that would make angels glad and that would bring into the fold of Christ thousands upon thousands who are now wandering in error" (GC 598.3).

"We should exert all the powers of the mind in the study of the Scriptures and should task the understanding to comprehend, as far as mortals can, the deep things of God; yet we must not forget that the docility and submission of a child is the true spirit of the learner. (GC 599.1)

Question: Returning to my friend the pastor's question regarding how we wear our hair or beards taken from Leviticus 19:27 and 21:5—yes, he is right; *it is* a statute [H2708]. *Many* among us ask, regarding some small command of God, is it important?

Answer: If it were not important, would God have required it?

Question: Does this apply to us today?

Answer: Does obedience apply to us today?

Question: What does the way we cut our hair or beard have to do with our salvation?

Answer: The degradation of the human race started with such questions in the minds of Adam and Eve. Our rationalization regarding what God expects of us and whether we live up to His expectations says more about us than it says about God and His Word. The idea that some requirement of God is too small for me to bother with tells God something about me. Individuals must not cherry-pick verses from the Scriptures to govern their lives; they must accept the Scriptures in their entirety. Otherwise, they are in rebellion.

The idea that God wants to be involved in the minutiae of our lives offends some people who continue to ask, "What does that have to do with salvation?" Salvation has to do with our *relationship* with God, and He wants to be involved in our lives in an intimate way, in every aspect of our lives, regardless of how that makes us appear to our worldly associates and maybe even because it makes us a *"peculiar people"* to those around us!

"Every chapter and every verse of the Bible is a communication from God to men. In place of the authority of the so-called fathers of the church, God bids us accept the word of the eternal Father, the Lord of heaven and earth. Here alone is truth unmixed with error. Let all who accept human authority, the customs of the church, or the traditions of the fathers, take heed to the warning conveyed in the words of Christ, 'In vain they do worship Me, teaching for doctrines the commandments of men' " (PP 504.3; see also DA 398.4).

"By obedience the people were to give evidence of their faith. So all who hope to be saved by the merits of the blood of Christ should realize that they themselves have something to do in securing their salvation. While it is Christ only that can redeem us from the penalty of transgression, we are to turn from sin to obedience. Man is to be saved by faith, not by works; yet his faith must be shown by his works. God has given His Son to die as a propitiation for sin, He has manifested the *light of truth*, the way of life, He has given *facilities*, *ordinances*, and *privileges*; and now man must *co-operate with these saving agencies;* he must appreciate and use the helps that God has provided—believe and obey all the divine requirements" (PP 279.1, emphasis added).

CHAPTER 21

SUMMATION

" 'Till heaven and earth pass,' said Jesus, 'one jot or one tittle shall in nowise pass from the law, till all be fulfilled.' By His own obedience to the law, Christ testified to its immutable character and proved that through His grace it could be perfectly obeyed by every son and daughter of Adam. On the mount He declared that not the smallest iota should pass from the law till all things should be accomplished— all things that concern the human race, all that relates to the plan of redemption. He does not teach that the law is ever to be abrogated, but He fixes the eye upon the utmost verge of man's horizon and assures us that until this point is reached the law will retain its authority so that none may suppose it was His mission to abolish the precepts of the law" (MB 49.3).

In Revelation 22:12–14, Jesus says, "And, behold, I come quickly; and my reward is with me, to give every man according as his work shall be. I am Alpha and Omega, the beginning and the end, the first and the last. Blessed are they that do his commandments [G1785], that they may have right to the tree of life, and may enter in through the gates into the city."

The word "commandments" [G1785] is the same word used in Matthew 5:19 to describe the "least commandments." It is also the same word used to describe the list of commandments essential for salvation, which included the statutes given by Jesus in Mark 10:19 and Matthew 19:17. This same word is used to describe the commandments that the saints keep in Revelation 14:12.

When John was in the Spirit on the Lord's day, he was told by the Alpha and Omega, "What thou seest, *write in a book* and send *it* to the seven churches" (Rev. 1:11). Paul, under the influence of the Holy Spirit, told Timothy, "All scripture is given by inspiration of God, and is profitable for doctrine, for reproof, for correction, for instruction in righteousness: that the man of God may be perfect [G739], thoroughly furnished unto all good works" (2 Tim. 3:16, 17).

In spite of this, we hear theologians tell us that "the laws of Moses" were nailed to the cross because they also *were written in a book*. Peter *warns* us about those who wrest [G4761], or pervert [derived from a Greek word meaning "to reverse," G4762] Scripture: "As also in all his [Paul] epistles, speaking in them of these things; in which are some things hard to be understood, which they that are unlearned and unstable wrest, as they do also the other scriptures, unto their own destruction" (2 Peter 3:16).

We endorse a biblical statute to support the view that people must pay tithe [Mal. 3:7, 8] to the church as a condition for salvation and, yet, we ignore the statutes that God says will mark the last-day message for planet earth in Malachi 4:4–6. God forbids usury, in Ezekiel 18:5–17, and yet; the church charges interest to the brethren, and trivializes other statutes which are required by God of His people.

"Because ye have said, We have made a covenant with death, and with hell are we at agreement; when the overflowing scourge shall pass through, it shall not come unto us: for we have made lies our refuge, and under falsehood have we hid ourselves: therefore thus saith the Lord GOD, Behold, I lay in Zion for a foundation a stone, a tried stone, a precious corner stone, a sure foundation: he that believeth shall not make haste. Judgment also will I lay to the line, and righteousness to the plummet: and the hail shall sweep away the refuge of lies, and the waters shall overflow the hiding place. And your covenant with death shall be disannulled, and your agreement with hell shall not stand; when the overflowing scourge shall pass through, then ye shall be trodden [see 2 Kings 9:33] down by it. From the time that it goeth forth it shall take you: for morning by morning shall it pass over, by day and by night: and it shall be a vexation ["fear," H2113] only to understand the *doctrine* [margin, King James Version]" (Isa. 28:15–19).

Christ says: "For had ye believed Moses, ye would have believed me; for he wrote of me. But if ye believe not his writings, how shall ye believe my words? I am Alpha and Omega, the beginning and the ending, saith the Lord, which is, and which was, and which is to come, the Almighty" (John 5:46, 47; Rev. 1:8).

What excuse shall we give Christ when He comes and asks: *Why did you not obey the laws I gave to Moses?*

"Therefore have I also made you contemptible and base before all the people, according as ye have not kept my ways, but have been *partial* in the law [*torah*]" (Mal. 2:9).

Ellen White said:

"Moses of himself framed no law. Christ, the angel whom God had appointed to go before his chosen people, gave to Moses *statutes* and *requirements necessary* to a living religion and to govern the people of God" (*Review and Herald*, May 6, 1875, par. 12).

"To day if ye will hear his voice, harden not your hearts, as in the provocation, in the day of temptation in the wilderness: when your fathers tempted me, proved me, and saw my works forty years. Wherefore I was grieved with that generation, and said, They do alway err in their heart; and they have not known my ways. So I sware in my wrath, They shall not enter into *my rest*" (Heb. 3:7–11).

Where did Israel tempt God? "Ye shall not tempt the LORD your God, as ye tempted him in Massah" (Deut. 6:16).

What was the remedy? "Ye shall diligently keep the commandments of the LORD your God, *and* His testimonies, *and* His statutes, which He hath commanded thee. And thou shalt *do* that which is right and good in the sight of the LORD: that it may be well with thee, and that thou mayest go in and possess the good land which the LORD sware unto thy fathers" (Deut. 6:17, 18).

"Men cannot with impunity reject the warning which God in mercy sends them. A message was sent from heaven to the world in Noah's day, and their salvation depended upon the manner in which they treated that message. Because they rejected the warning, the Spirit of God was withdrawn from the sinful race, and they perished in the waters of the Flood. In the time of Abraham, mercy ceased to plead with the guilty inhabitants of Sodom, and all but Lot with his wife and two daughters were consumed by the fire sent down from heaven. So in the days of Christ. The Son of God declared to the unbelieving Jews of that generation: 'Your house is left unto you desolate.' Matthew 23:38. Looking down to the last days, the same Infinite Power declares, concerning those who 'received not the love of the truth, that they might be saved': 'For this cause God shall send them strong delusion, that they should believe a lie: that they all might be damned who believed not the truth, but had pleasure in unrighteousness.' 2 Thessalonians 2:10–12. As they reject the teachings of His word, God withdraws His Spirit and leaves them to the deceptions which they love" (GC 431.1).

Note: The rejection of the message from God results in the Spirit of God being withdrawn.

If this matter of being faithful to the *entire law* still strikes you as not being required, turn the page.

CHAPTER 22

FINAL WARNING

Special Message for the Stubborn and Rebellious

"One thing it is certain is soon to be realized the great apostasy, which is developing and increasing and waxing stronger, and will continue to do so until the Lord shall descend from heaven with a shout. We are to hold fast the *first principles* of our denominated faith, and go forward from strength to increased faith. Ever we are to keep the faith that has been substantiated by the Holy Spirit of God from the *earlier events* of our experience, until the present time. …

"We are to see and realize the importance of the message, made certain by its divine origin. We are to follow on to know the Lord, that we may know that His going forth is prepared as the morning.

"Have not the hearts of Christ's disciples burned within them as He has talked with us by the way and opened to us the Scriptures? Has not the Lord Jesus opened to us the Scriptures, and presented to us things kept secret from the foundation of the world? *Some have heard the reading of the evidence of the binding claims of the law of God*, and the enjoined obedience to his commandments, and have felt their characters to be in such contrast to the requirements that *had* they been placed in circumstances similar to Jehoiakim, king of Judah, they would have done as he did. A special message was sent to him to be read in his hearing, but after listening to three or four pages, he cut it out with a penknife, and cast it into the fire. But this could not destroy the message; for the word of God will never return unto him void. The same Holy Spirit who had given the first testimony, which was refused and burned, came to the servant of God, who caused the first to be written in the roll, and repeated the very message that had been rejected, caused the latter to be written and added a great deal more to it" (*The New York Indicator*, Feb. 7, 1906).

"The Jewish leaders thought themselves too wise to need instruction, too righteous to need salvation, too highly honored to need the honor that comes from Christ. The Saviour turned from them to entrust to others the privileges they had abused and the work they had slighted. God's glory must be revealed, His word established. Christ's kingdom must be set up in the world" (AA 16.1).

"Having committed themselves to a course of opposition to Christ, every act of resistance became to the priests an additional incentive to pursue the same course. Their obstinacy became more and more determined. It was not that they could not yield; they could, but would not. It was not alone because they were guilty and deserving of death, not alone because they had put to death the Son of God, that they were cut off from salvation; it was because they armed themselves with opposition to God. They persistently rejected light and stifled the convictions of the Spirit. The influence that controls the children of disobedience worked in them, leading them to abuse the men through whom God was working. The malignity of their rebellion was intensified by each successive act of resistance against God and the message He had given His servants to declare. Every day, in their refusal to repent, the Jewish leaders took up their rebellion afresh, preparing to reap that which they had sown.

"The wrath of God is not declared against unrepentant sinners merely because of the sins they have committed, but because, when called to repent, they choose to continue in resistance, repeating the sins of the past in defiance of the light given them. If the Jewish leaders had submitted to the convicting power of the Holy Spirit, they would have been pardoned; but they were determined not to yield. In the same way, the sinner, by continued resistance, places himself where the Holy Spirit cannot influence him" (AA 61.2; 62.1).

"Those who are willing to have the straight, plain messages of God consumed, to get them out of their sight, will only give increased publicity to, and confirmation of, the messages they dismissed and repulsed. When the Lord sends a message to any man or woman, and they refused to be corrected, refuse to receive it, that is not the end of the message by any means. All the transaction is recorded, and those who took part in it, by their refusal to be corrected, pronounce their own sentence against themselves" (*Special Testimonies*, Series B, No.7, p. 59.1).

"When God sends a message to any person, minister or doctor, if men pursue a course to make of no effect the message sent, a course that destroys the influence of the message that God designed should make a change in the principles of the one corrected, and turn his heart to repentance, it would be better for these men if they had never been born" (*Special Testimonies*, Series B, No. 7, p. 59, par. 2).

"So when God's judgments shall fall upon the earth before its deluge by fire, the impenitent will know just where and what their sin is—the despising of His holy law. Yet they will have no more true repentance than did the old-world sinners" (PP 99.3).

"The thing that hath been, it is that which shall be; and that which is done is that which shall be done: and there is no new thing under the sun" (Eccles. 1:9).

"We dare not tamper with God's word, dividing His holy law; calling one portion essential and another nonessential, to gain the favor of the world. The Lord whom we serve is able to deliver us. Christ has conquered the powers of earth; and shall we be afraid of a world already conquered?" (GC 610.1).

In this book, I have written about laws found in Scripture. I have included warnings against disobedience and the results of stubbornness and resistance to God's Word, and I have included some of the joys to be had with complete surrender to God's will. Sin is a terrible thing. It separates us from the Father. The enemy of souls understands that fact oh so well. Nevertheless, while he has lost the war, he wants to take us with him and break God's heart.

In Isaiah, God speaks of the end of sinners, yet He offers hope to those who repent.

"Therefore as the fire devoureth the stubble, and the flame consumeth the chaff, so their root shall be as rottenness, and their blossom shall go up as dust: because they have cast away the law of the LORD of hosts, and despised the word of the Holy One of Israel. Therefore is the anger of the LORD kindled against his people, and he hath stretched forth his hand against them, and hath smitten them: and the hills did tremble, and their carcases [were] torn in the midst of the streets. For all this his anger is not turned away, but his hand is stretched out still" (Isa. 5:24, 25, emphasis added).

Four more times in Isaiah, God states that His hand is stretched out still. Then, at the very end of the book, He declares: "I have spread out my hands all the day unto a rebellious people, which walketh in a way [that was] not good, after their *own* thoughts" (Isa. 65:2).

Paul reminds us of God's patience: "All day long I have stretched forth my hands unto a disobedient and gainsaying people" (Rom. 10:21). God still has His hands stretched out! Don't pass up this opportunity!

TEACH Services, Inc.
P U B L I S H I N G

We invite you to view the complete
selection of titles we publish at:
www.TEACHServices.com

We encourage you to write us
with your thoughts about this,
or any other book we publish at:
info@TEACHServices.com

TEACH Services' titles may be purchased in
bulk quantities for educational, fund-raising,
business, or promotional use.
bulksales@TEACHServices.com

Finally, if you are interested in seeing
your own book in print, please contact us at:
publishing@TEACHServices.com

We are happy to review your manuscript at no charge.

www.ingramcontent.com/pod-product-compliance
Lightning Source LLC
Chambersburg PA
CBHW070553160426
43199CB00014B/2490